# Chapter & Verse

## Crosswords And Other Puzzles

### ~ Bible Study ~

# Chapter & Verse

## Crosswords And Other Puzzles

### ~ Genesis, Book Two ~

*by tjjohnson*

AuthorHouse™
1663 Liberty Drive
Bloomington, IN 47403
www.authorhouse.com
Phone: 1-800-839-8640

First published by AuthorHouse 12/29/2009

ISBN: 978-1-4490-5129-7 (sc)

Printed in the United States of America
Bloomington, Indiana

This book is printed on acid-free paper.

## Dedication

*This book is dedicated to people
who love Bible study; and to those
brave souls who took a chance on
My first puzzle book.*

*Thank You.*

*I appreciate all the feedback
which has provided me with
a variety of insights and ideas for
Future books.*

*I wish you God's Continued Favor,
and His Everlasting Peace!*

# HELPFUL HINTS

All Bible References are from
The King James Study Bible
You will need a concordance, a Bible Dictionary
And/Or use of a computer for access to
Web-based Bible research.


To find correct squares for crossword puzzle entries,
read the puzzle numbers from left to right,
Horizontally, line by line,
whether the clue is Across or Down


(Ch) is used to indicate Chapter
(V) is used to indicate Verse of puzzle reference Chapter


Of twenty-five puzzles,
Eleven are formatted to benefit left-handers:
Pages 12, 18, 26, 28, 30, 42, 48, 50, 52, 56, and 58

# ~ Acknowledgements ~

Special recognition to:
Pastor Timothy J. Winters, D.Min.
Under-Shepherd to God's people at Bayview Baptist Church
in San Diego for the past 36 years.
Where I learned to use and develop my gifts
as a Bible teacher and writer.

Sister Betty J. Winters,
first lady of Bayview who
proofread my first drafts,
and offered valuable feedback on my writing.

Carolyn Denese Wright, who has a special gift of exhortation,
and intuitively knows when a person needs building up.
She always has kind and encouraging words
to help keep me motivated and productive.

Carrie Alexander, my long-time friend,
stoked my writer's senses years ago.
She planted the seed in me
to use the gift that comes rather naturally.

Ruthie Wilson, who provides occasional photography;
Bill Harris and Reverend Peter Zindler, who helped critique my work;
And, Sharon Cawthorne who contributed helpful marketing ideas.

# TABLE OF CONTENTS

# ~ PUZZLE CONTENTS CONTINUED~

# ~ APPENDIX A ~

## PUZZLE ANSWERS

# ~ APPENDIX A ANSWERS
## CONTINUED ~

# INTRODUCTION

These puzzles are designed as an aid for studying individual chapters of the Bible, and at the same time, providing an enjoyable activity. They offer an excellent way to review a chapter you've read; thereby increasing the probability of retaining Bible facts and building your Biblical knowledge.

Each puzzle is based on chapters taken from *The King James Study Bible*. In reading and solving the puzzles, you will encounter certain words and phrases you think you understand. **However, it is advisable to use a good Bible Dictionary and concordance for Hebrew and Greek translations** even for common words, because in presentation of Biblical stories and situations, words that we use everyday often have a completely different connotation. Word usage and translation also depend heavily on how the word is used in each occurrence. You can find Bible discussions and word interpretations on various Bible study web pages on the Internet. In writing this book, time and time again, I found myself depending heavily on http://www.blueletterbible.org and other Bible-based websites for word translations. *The King James Study Bible* also provides word translations for selected word usage.

Puzzles in this book review Genesis 26 through 50, and includes chapters that were not incorporated in *Chapter & Verse, Crosswords and Other Puzzles, Genesis Book One*. I hope you will enjoy solving these puzzles as much as I have enjoyed writing them. And I pray they accomplish that which they're designed to do—help you study and learn the Bible.

May God continue to make His Face to shine upon you,

tjjohnson

*Now,*
*Write it before them*
*In a table,*
*And note it in a*
*Book*
*That it may be for*
*Time…*
*To come…*
*For ever, And…*
*Ever.*

*From Isaiah 30:8*

Chapter & Verse

# People and Other Characters of Genesis
## Various Scripture,
### (KJV)

**These words are found in the puzzle grid on following page:**

| | | |
|---|---|---|
| Abel | Isaac | Rachel |
| Abimelech | Ishmael | Rebekah |
| Abraham | Jacob | Sarah |
| | | |
| Adam | Joseph | Schemer |
| Angels | Judah | Serpent |
| Butler | Laban | Seth |
| | | |
| Cain | Leah | Shem |
| Dreamer | Lot | Shepherd |
| Enoch | Ham | Pharaoh |
| | | |
| Esau | Melchizedek | Potiphar |
| God | MrsPotiphar | Tamar |
| Hagar | Noah | TJJohnson |

## People and Other Characters of Genesis
### Various Scripture, (KJV)

The characters below form words found on the previous page. Find and circle the words in the grid. Words can go across left to right, up and down, and in three diagonals. Various words not pertaining to the puzzle may be found in the grid. Words may also appear more than once.

```
M  J  N  F  L  L  H  A  B  I  M  E  L  E  C  H  V  D  N  S
M  Z  U  W  H  C  Y  I  T  J  J  O  H  N  S  O  N  K  N  A
E  T  Z  D  O  L  S  S  L  D  R  E  A  M  E  R  M  A  Y  R
L  P  A  N  A  L  H  H  N  S  E  R  P  E  N  T  B  K  D  A
C  O  E  M  T  H  E  M  R  M  L  E  A  H  Y  A  M  O  N  H
H  T  L  L  A  M  M  A  B  H  M  P  F  N  L  W  G  B  J  G
I  I  L  K  C  R  T  E  A  D  A  M  J  X  X  Q  S  Z  Y  J
Z  P  O  V  L  N  M  L  J  L  N  E  M  R  X  D  X  E  Y  Z
E  H  T  D  I  N  G  L  N  A  M  M  V  T  R  K  R  K  T  F
D  A  Z  A  N  N  H  W  T  W  C  W  N  E  J  A  H  W  D  H
E  R  C  I  S  A  A  C  H  W  S  O  H  M  H  A  T  R  B  D
K  K  J  D  P  Q  Y  M  M  L  T  Z  B  P  K  W  E  M  H
R  L  H  T  E  H  H  N  E  T  Z  B  I  E  Z  H  A  R  A  M
D  A  P  K  S  D  A  G  K  Q  Z  T  B  R  P  H  R  B  M  W
L  F  C  D  A  T  N  R  D  M  O  E  E  E  A  E  K  B  M  M
T  R  H  H  U  A  N  L  A  P  R  M  H  R  L  L  D  X  N  P
B  C  Y  Y  E  K  F  O  S  O  E  S  B  T  D  L  G  R  G  C
N  J  P  K  N  L  M  R  A  H  H  A  U  L  R  W  R  J  N  N
J  O  S  E  P  H  M  M  C  H  M  B  H  Q  R  Q  V  M  K  K
R  V  H  A  G  A  R  S  Z  Q  Z  A  B  E  L  T  W  G  M  Y
```

Chapter & Verse

**Places and Cases in Genesis**
**Various Scripture**
**(KJV)**

**Find and circle these words in the grid on the following page:**

| | | |
|---|---|---|
| Altar | Famine | Nile |
| Angels | Flood | Padanaram |
| Battles | Gaza | |
| | | |
| Beersheba | Gerar | Sacrifice |
| Beginning | Gilead | Salem |
| Bethel | Gomorrah | |
| | | |
| Canaan | Goshen | Seir |
| Dothan | Haran | Serpent |
| Dreamer | Heaven | |
| | | |
| Earth | Kings | Shepherd |
| Eden | Hebron | Sodom |
| Edom | Jehovahjireh | |
| | | |
| Egypt | Kadesh | Succoth |
| Ephrath | Machpelah | Tithes |
| Euphrates | Mesopotamia | TJJohnson |

## Places and Cases in Genesis
### Various Scripture, (KJV)

The characters below form words found on the previous page. Find and circle the words in the grid. Words can go across from left to right, up and down, and in three diagonals. Various words not pertaining to the puzzle may be found in the grid, and some words may appear more than once.

```
T  S  S  L  G  M  M  X  S  Q  P  T  F  N  P  R  L  R  K  W  N
I  A  E  T  H  R  H  E  N  H  S  K  O  N  E  Z  H  K  Z  A  R
T  C  R  V  T  L  F  M  S  E  E  R  F  M  Q  D  F  Y  R  K  Z
H  R  P  E  R  A  M  K  T  O  B  P  A  A  C  Y  O  A  T  G  K
E  I  E  X  D  E  L  A  Z  E  P  E  H  B  M  F  H  M  M  V  K
S  F  N  Q  L  E  R  T  H  M  R  O  R  E  M  I  R  Y  W  J  K
Z  I  T  A  F  H  N  K  A  D  D  R  T  W  R  C  N  H  J  E  A
Q  C  S  P  P  B  E  D  Z  R  G  E  R  A  R  D  A  E  T  H  D
A  E  N  U  D  E  G  O  N  P  C  M  C  T  M  L  T  N  Y  O  E
N  N  E  Z  D  T  Y  T  Q  I  D  R  N  J  E  I  R  Q  A  V  S
M  G  G  O  N  H  P  H  L  Q  L  F  V  P  H  R  A  B  D  A  H
N  K  O  E  W  E  T  A  D  L  H  E  H  A  S  M  Q  K  F  H  N
S  L  L  R  L  L  R  N  L  T  K  C  R  G  O  S  H  E  N  J  R
F  U  N  X  S  K  M  R  H  A  R  N  E  N  R  J  M  T  I  P
R  U  C  G  I  L  E  A  D  M  O  I  N  P  P  S  T  C  K  R  M
F  R  H  C  Y  K  E  J  R  M  K  Y  G  F  J  H  A  F  K  E  D
P  K  V  T  O  R  L  K  O  M  H  E  A  V  E  N  R  L  X  H  G
S  O  D  O  M  T  P  G  T  J  J  O  H  N  S  O  N  A  E  B  A
L  Y  S  E  I  R  H  N  M  B  A  T  T  L  E  S  K  T  T  M  Z
P  B  E  G  I  N  N  I  N  G  R  Y  N  D  N  M  K  C  K  H  A
B  E  E  R  S  H  E  B  A  Z  P  A  D  A  N  A  R  A  M  X  V
```

# God's Promises To Abraham
## Genesis 12:1-13, 14:18; 15:1-6, 12-13, (KJV)

**Across**:

2. Father of Abram.
5. God told Abram to walk the length and _____ of the land.
9. And so Abram _____ in the LORD, (to 15D).
10. A common suffix for the people who lived in Canaan, (plural).
12. And his _____ would also be great, (from 44A).
14. Curse those that _____ thee.
16. God promised to make Abram's seed as the _____ of the earth.
19. And _____ in every direction, (from 24D).
22. So Abram _____ Haran as God instructed him to do.
23. God told Abram to leave his _____.
25. In every _____, the land would belong to Abraham's and his descendants.
28. And thou _____ a blessing, (2 wds).
30. Sarai's name was later changed to _____.
32. Eliezer was Abram's _____.
34. (From 3D) ... and to the west of _____.
35. Abram built an _____ to honor God and His promise.
37. The caravan traveled through this city.
39. And God said he would _____ Abram the place where he should go, (from 21D).
41. Abram did not leave all his family; _____ traveled with him.
43. Abram was seventy _____ years old when he left his relatives.
42. Bless those that bless _____.
44. Abram was destined to become a great _____, (to 12A).
45. God told Abram that his seed would be as the _____ of heaven.
47. God's word to Abram was a _____.

**Down:**

1. "I am thy _____," (to 7D).
3. Abram continued to a mountain to the _____ of Bethel, (to 34A).
4. Another translation of descendant, (ch 12:7). [1]
5. The Lord _____ thee and keep thee, (Num 6:24).
6. God caused Abram to fall into a _____ sleep.
7. "And, [I am] thy exceeding great _____," (from 1D).
8. The land grant covered the area from the _____ River to the river Euphrates.
11. God told Abram his seed would be as a _____ in a land that wasn't theirs.
13. Abram traveled way south toward _____.
14. Puzzle content was _____ by tjjohnson.
15. (From 9A) ...and God _____ it toward him for Righteousness.
17. A stranger can be described as a _____, (ch 15:13). [2]
18. Israel (Abram's seed) would be in bondage _____ hundred years.
20. Lot was Abram's _____.
21. Abram was urged to go to a _____, (to 39A).
24. God told Abram to _____ up his eyes, (to 19A).
26. The land promised to Abram's children was the land of the _____, (singular).
27. Man would not be able to _____ the seed of Abram.
29. God told Abram to look toward _____.

(Continued at bottom of puzzle, next page)

# God's Promises To Abraham

31. He was called a friend of God, Is 41:8; Jam 2:23.
33. "All _____ shall be blessed in thee."
36. Abram took his _____, and everything he had, to go where God would lead him.
38. The name of Abram's brother who died.
40. Abram packed his _____ and other possessions to prepare for his journey.
43. The Lord told Abram to _____ not.
46. Puzzle author is _____ Johnson.

[1] 4D    Wayne A. Brindle, et al. eds., *The King James Study Bible* (Lynchburg, VA: Liberty University, 1988) p. 30;
[2] 17D    http://www.blueletterbible.org

Chapter & Verse

**Faith, Hope, Trust**
**Believing God's Promises**
**Genesis 12:1-9; Heb 10:1-16; 11:1-3 (KJV)**

**(Note: To find the correct places for each answer, read the puzzle numbers from left to right, horizontally, line by line, whether the clue is Across or Down.)**

**Across:**
3. If God said it, He will ___ it.
6. Souls in 12:5 refer to _____.
7. This book of puzzles was _____ for Bible study by answer to (11 Across).
10. Lot was Abraham's _____.
11. Author of puzzle content is _____.
14. When Abram's families left on their journey, they took ____ their possessions.
15. Lot's father, (Gen 11:27).
17. One can not believe God unless you _____ Him.
18. God promised to make Abraham a great _____.
19. In the Bible, this word often refers to heir/s or descendant/s.
21. God told Abraham to leave his _____ house.
23. This is the land God promised to Abraham and his heirs.
25. The family of ____ also traveled with Abraham.
26. Before he was Abraham, he was _____.
30. Noah built an ark without evidence of _____, (Gen 2:5; 6:13-17; 7:4).
31. God promised to make Abraham's _____ great.
32. Many forefathers of Israel _____ without seeing the promise fulfilled, (Heb 10:13-16).
34. Faith means that we don't have to ____ something to believe it.
35. Abram built an altar unto the LORD in Shechem and in _____, (Gen 12:7-8).
38. Many _____ accompanied Abraham as he traveled.
39. To have faith is to _____.
42. The land where Abraham traveled was described as a _____ land.
43. '...and thou shall be a _____.'
45. Abraham's father worshipped ____ gods, (Joshua 24:2).
47. (From 41D) '_____ those that curse thee.'
48. Abraham's wife was called _____before she was named Sarah.
49. Both names of Abraham's wife can be translated as _____. [1].
51. When God told Abraham and Sarah of their future son they both _____.
52. Abraham translates as _____ of a Multitude. [2]
53. Abraham left everything to ____ where God had destined for him to go.
54. Heb 11:3 says through faith we _____.
55. Also spelled Shechem.

**Down:**
1. To have _____ is to have faith.
2. Sarah was to become the _____ of many nations, (Gen 17:16).
4. The proper name of God.
5. To exercise our faith, we must often take some _____.

(Continued on page 11)

# Faith, Hope, Trust, Believing God's Promises
## Genesis 12:1-9; Heb 11:1-3 (KJV)

**(Read numbers from left to right, line by line, to find correct spaces for answers)**

**Faith...**

**Hope...**

**Trust...**

**Faith...**

What is it?

That is truly a question to ponder

Can we surely know what God intended?

I, sometimes wonder.

The **Substance** of things...

Many... many...things..., Hoped for...

The **Evidence** of things...,

Endless...things,

Unseen? (From Heb 11:1)

**Hope...**

An Expectation of...

Anticipation of...

Trusting that...

Something..., actually is—will be,

Exactly what you believe it to be.

**Trust...**

A Deep and inner Knowing,

Confidence that what you believe

to be true,

Is actually, Already true...

Now..., and in the future.

**Faith then...**

Is Hoping...Expecting...,

Trusting...Knowing,

Confident... Certain,

Convinced...Assured,

Believing.

**Faith, Hope, Trust (Down: Continued from page 8):**

8. Down south of Bethel lies _____.
9. Abraham's father, (Gen 11:31).
12. Heb 11:1 says that part of having faith is the conviction of things _____, (2 wds).
13. '...and in thee, all the families of the earth shall be _____.'
16. The LORD _____ unto Abram in the plain of Moreh.
20. Another word for family is _____.
22. Besides leaving his father's family, God told Abraham to leave his _____.
24. They occupied the land promised to Abraham and his heirs, (plural).
26. Forefather of the Jews, and the Arabs.
27. Abram means _____ or High Father.[3]
28. When he began this journey to follow God, Abraham was _____ years old, (2 wds).
29. One must believe that God _____.
33. Jehovah, the _____ One.[4]
36. Hebrew translation of _____ is Y@hovah.[5]
37. Before this city was Bethel, it was _____, (Gen 28:19).
40. Abraham's _____ had land named after him, (Gen 11:27-32).
41. God said He would '_____ those that bless thee, and...' (to 47A)
42. She gave birth to Isaac when she was ninety years old, (Gen 17:17).
44. Bethel translates to House of _____.[6]
46. Obeying God, Abraham left the city of _____.
47. Ur, the land of Abram's father, was located in _____ (Gen 11:28-31).
48. Isaac was Abraham's _____ son.
50. God told Abraham that He would _____ him the land that would be his.
52. Without this, it is impossible to please God, (Heb 11:6).

[1] 49A    T. Alton Bryant, Zondervan ed., *The New Compact Bible Dictionary* (Grand Rapids: Zondervan, 1967), p.525.

[2] 52A    http://www.blueletterbible.org

[3] 27D    ibid.

[4] 33D    ibid.

[5] 36D    ibid.

[6] 44D    ibid.

Chapter & Verse

# Battle of the Kings
## Genesis 14
### (KJV),

**(Note: To find the correct space for each answer, read the numbers from left to right, line by line, horizontally, whether the clue is Across or Down.)**

## Battle of the Kings
## Genesis 14, (KJV)

**Across**:

1.  Abram was of _____ lineage.
3.  Puzzle author's name.
7.  Amraphel was king of _____.
10. Abram refused to take any _____ of the war.
13. The _____ and Amorites were among those attacked.
17. A tenth part.
18. The kings in verse one waged _____ against the kings of verse two.
21. Siddim is also called _____ Sea.
23. Melchizedek found only _____ in the Old Testament.
25. Jesus Christ, a priest after the _____ of Melchizedek.
26. Abram dwelt in the plain of Mamre, which is in_____, (Gen 13:18).
27. These quiz questions are from the book of _____.
29. King Bera went out to meet the returning makeshift _____.
34. Mamre was of the _____ people.
35. Salem translates as _____.[1]
37. Melchizedek was described as _____ of the most high God.
38. Aber, Eschol, and Mamre were allies _____ Abram.
40. God delivered the enemy into the _____ of Abram and his men.
43. Testament translates as _____.[2]
45. The kings of Sodom and Gomorrah _____ into the pits.
46. _____ was captured by the attacking kings.
48. Birsha was king of _____.
51. The revolting cities had served King Chedorlaomer for _____ years.
52. Melchizedek was king of _____.
54. En-mishpat is also called _____, (v7).
56. Four kings were fighting against _____ kings.
57. The leader king had _____ allies in verse one.
58. The king of Salem brought bread and _____ to Abram.
59. Abram gave_____ to King Melchizedek.

**Down**:

2.  Melchizedek _____ Abram.
4.  Lot and his family lived in the plain of _____.
5.  King Bera of Sodom offered the captured _____ to Abram.
6.  Five _____ are named in verse two.
8.  _____ translates as cave dweller, (Look up proper nouns in v6). [3]
9.  He had been the leader among other kings until they rebelled against him.
11. Abram armed his _____ to hunt down the attacking kings.
12. Seir translates as_____ or shaggy. [4]

(Continued on next page)

**Battle of the Kings: Continued:**
**Down:**

14. He was king of nations.
15. Smote (verses 5, 7, 15) can be defined as _____. [5]
16. King and priest in this chapter characterize the law of first _____.
19. The Horites were attacked in Mount _____.
20. Abram would only accept food for his young _____ from the king of Sodom.
22. His name would later be changed to Abraham.
24. Allies also know as _____.
28. Utter defeat, (see v17). [6]
29. Slime also referred to as _____.
30. The city of Noah's son, _____, was also attacked.
31. The king of Bela.
32. Lot was Abram's _____.
33. Victuals are provisions called this.
36. Chedorlaomer was king of _____.
39. Abram's army pursued the enemy unto Hobah, which is _____ of Damascus.
41. The vale of Siddim was full of these pits.
42. _____ kings are named in verse one.
44. Confederate in verse 13 translates as _____. [7]
47. New Testament references for Melchisedec found in _____.
49. Abram refused gifts so King Bera could not boast about making him _____.
50. Siddim was located in a _____.
53. The place where the kings gathered.
55. Seir is in the land of _____. [8]

---

[1] 35A  http://www.blueletterbible.org

[2] 43A  http://net.bible.org

[3] 8D  ibid

[4] 12D  ibid

[5] 15D  Wayne A. Brindle, et al. eds., *The King James Study Bible* (Lynchburg, VA: Liberty University, 1988) pp. 32-33

[6] 28D  ibid

[7] 44D  ibid

[8] 55D  Alton, Bryant T., ed., *The New Compact Bible Dictionary* (Grand Rapids: Zondervan, 1967) p. 532

## Abraham and Abimelech
## Genesis 20, (KJV)

**(Puzzle Grid on page 17)**
**Across:**
4. Father of a _____; Hebrew translation of Abraham.
5. _____ same as or.
6. 'A lodging place' is the definition of _____, (look up city of v1). [1]
7. God told the king that Abraham was a _____.
9. Initials of author _____.
12. God conveyed to Abimelech that he was a _____ man.
15. Abram, or _____.
19. Fear can be described or defined as _____.
20. 'A covering of the eyes' was a gesture meaning to _____ Sarah from reproach, (v16).
21. The king gave Abraham a thousand pieces of _____.
24. Abimelech got up _____ in the morning after his troubled sleep.
25. Abimelech's sin would have been against _____, not Abraham.
26. On _____ of my wife, same as 'For my wife's sake.'
28. Reproved in verse sixteen refers to being _____. [2]
30. Abraham used the same _____ with Abimelech as he had with Pharaoh earlier.
31. In early Bible history, some men had more than one _____.
33. Gerar lay south of _____.
37. Sarah was Abraham's wife as well as his half _____.
39. God stopped the king from _____.
40. Feminine pronoun.
42. Kadesh is located _____ of Shur.
43. Kadesh, same as Kadesh-_____.
45. It is said that _____ of loose change or coins were not yet discovered; money was weighed.
46. Abraham asked _____ to say he was her brother.
48. Abraham left the _____ of Mamre and traveled south.
50. Sarah and Abraham had the same _____.
51. God _____ death to the king and all his possessions.
52. Because he was _____, Abraham said Sarah was his sister.
53. God has a plural and singular _____.

**Down:**
1. The king took Sarah into his _____.
2. Abimelech, _____ of Gerar.
3. Abraham did not think the people of Gerar _____ God.
7. Abraham _____ for Abimelech and his household.
8. Gerar was an ancient _____ post.
10. As he had done with Pharaoh, God _____ before the king claimed Sarah as his wife.
11. 'She is a man's wife' means she is _____.

(Continued on next page)

## Abraham and Abimelech Continued:

### Down:

13. Abimelech expressed to God that he was _____.
14. Hebrew translation of Kadesh. [3]
16. In early Bible history, God permitted close relatives to _____.
17. Sore afraid can be stated as _____ afraid.
18. Shur is first mentioned in Gen 16:7 in reference to Sarai's _____, (could be 2 wds).
22. The _____ healed Abimelech.
23. Abraham had _____ to dwell anywhere on Abimelech's land.
27. You and I, us or _____.
28. Abraham _____ south and stopped in Gerar.
29. God caused the _____ of all the women in the king's house to be closed.
31. Hebrew meaning for Shur is _____. [4]
32. 'My father is _____' is the Hebrew translation of Abimelech. [5]
34. Translation for 'Exalted or High father', (look up names, Gen 17:5). [6]
35. In his apology, the king _____ Abraham.
36. Abimelech gave Abraham more _____.
38. Shur is located to the _____ of where Abraham had previously lodged.
41. King Abimelech's experience sounds more like a _____ than a dream.
42. A city near southern Palestine, also called Kadesh, (Gen 14:7).
43. Abimelech told Sarah that her _____ was a 'covering of the eyes.'
44. We are all descendants of _____.
47. The word 'pieces' in verse 16 indicates that it has been _____ to the original text of the Bible.
49. The king's _____ showed him the truth about Sarah.

[1] 6A  http://www.blueletterbible.org

[2] 28A  Wayne A. Brindle, et al. eds., *The King James Study Bible*, (Lynchburg, VA: Liberty University, 1988), p. 43

[3] 14D  http://www.blueletterbible.org

[4] 31D  ibid

[5] 32D  ibid

[6] 34D  ibid

# Abraham and Abimelech
## Genesis 20, (KJV)

**(Read numbers from left to right, line by line, to find correct spaces for answers)**

Chapter & Verse

**Isaac & Abimelech**
**Genesis 26, (KJV)**

**(Read the numbers from left to right, line by line, horizontally, whether the clue is Across or Down.)**

**Isaac & Abimelech**
**Genesis 26, (KJV)**

**(Ch is used for Chapter of same book; V is for Verse of puzzle reference chapter)**

**Across:**

1. The Philistines realized the _____ of the LORD towards Isaac.
4. Because Abraham obeyed the _____ of the Lord, we are all blessed.
7. The king decreed _____ to any man who touched Rebekah.
9. Fair to look at.
10. A translation for Shebah, oath or _____, (v33).[1]
12. Translation of sporting (v8).[2]
14. Isaac reaped one_____ fold of whatever he sowed in Gerar.
18. Well of the Oath (v33) translates as _____.[3]
20. The Philistines _____ Isaac.
21. Betimes (v31) translates as _____.[4]
22. Primary place of action of this story is _____.
26. Puzzle content created by _____.
27. King Abimelech asked Isaac to _____ the country.
28. Isaac _____ about his wife just as his father had.
29. The people and the land were experiencing a _____ during this time.
32. Isaac prepared a _____ for King Abimelech and his captain, (v30).
33. God told _____ not to fear; the same thing He had told Abraham.
35. Egypt was considered to be _____ from where Isaac journeyed.
36. Seed, as in one's family line.[5]
41. Ordinarily, a king took any woman he wanted for a _____, or concubine, (to 58A).
42. Name of well in verse 21.
43. God made an _____ with Abraham to give land to Isaac.
45. The men of Gerar stopped up or _____ the wells which Abraham had dug.
46. Abraham lost a well in the same _____ as Isaac did, (Gen 21:25).
47. Your homeland is the same as your _____.
50. King Abimelech was king of the _____.
52. The name given to the well near an altar Isaac built.
54. The king saw Isaac _____ with Rebekah, (to 2D).
55. Many _____ passed between Abraham's visit to the Philistine country and his son's visit.
56. Seemingly common name of a Philistine king.
57. Sitnah (v21) translates as strife or _____.[6]
58. (From 41A)... as long as she was not _____.
59. Isaac's reason for calling his wife his sister was the _____ one that his father had used.

**(Down:** Clues on next page)

## Isaac & Abimelech
## Genesis 26, (KJV)

**(Down Continued)**:

2. (From 54A) ... and realized Isaac's _____ to trick him.
3. Isaac had many _____ and herds, and flocks.
5. 'Of a surety' in verse nine can be translated as _____.[7]
6. Isaac also built an _____ in the place where God spoke to him about his blessing.
8. Isaac and his _____ had similar experiences with the Abimelechs.
11. God _____ Isaac not to go to Egypt.
13. Esek (v20) translates as _____, or Contention.[8]
15. The Rehoboth well was not _____ by the men of Gerar, (v22).
16. Same as springing water, (v19).[9]
17. There was also a famine at the time when _____ dealt with King Abimelech.
19. Abram went to _____ because of a famine, (Gen 12:10).
23. Isaac's wife, (Genesis spelling).
24. Waxed translated is same as _____ (v13).[10]
25. Chief Captain of the Philistine army.
30. The chief captain had the same _____ as one who had bargained with Abraham, (Gen 21:22).
31. This Abimelech was not the same _____ that Abraham dealt with.
34. Isaac dug _____ well in the area of the altar.
37. Name of Isaac's well in the valley.
38. A treaty (v28) can be said to be a _____.[11]
39. The king and his captain wanted to make a _____.
40. Translation of _____ is wide places or spaciousness, (v22).[12]
44. If a king wanted another man's wife, he was likely to _____ the husband, (2 Sam 11:1-17).
45. 'Went forward' in verse 13 means Isaac continued to _____.[13]
48. Alternate spelling of Rebekah, (Rom 9:10).
49. The LORD promised Isaac that He would be with him, and _____ him.
51. The king's wives were part of his _____.
53. From the _____ of Abraham, every nation on earth would be blessed.

[1] Merrill F. Unger, *Unger's Bible Dictionary,* Third Edition (Chicago: Moody Press, 1966), p. 1007
[2-13] Wayne A. Brindle, et al. eds., *The King James Study Bible*, (Lynchburg, VA: Liberty University, 1988), pp. 54-55

## Birthrights & Blessings
## Genesis 27 – 28, (KJV)

**(Ch is used for Chapter of same book; V is used for Verse of puzzle chapter)**

**Across:**
2. Isaac commanded that Jacob not marry a woman of _____, (to 33D).
4. All the families of the earth would be _____ through Jacob.
6. Isaac was forty years old when he _____ Rebekah.
8. (From 10A), Lying would surely bring one a _____ not a blessing.
9. Esau _____ to kill Jacob after Isaac died.
10. _____ was uneasy about lying to his father because..., (to 8A).
11. Esau's skin was very _____.
12. (From 25D) ...because he promised to give the land to Jacob and his _____, (28:10-15).
13. Esau married a daughter of _____ because he knew it would displease his parents.
15. Jacob was _____ skinned.
17. Laban lived in the town of _____.
20. Rebekah's father was of _____ descent.
21. Isaac sent Jacob to live with Rebekah's father _____.
23. (From 35A), so Isaac wanted to feel the _____ of the son he was talking with, (27:21).
24. One night Jacob dreamed of a great _____ that reached into the heavens, (to 18D).
26. As Isaac and Jacob talked, Isaac asked Jacob to _____ him, (to 51A).
28. Jacob promised to give God a _____ of all that God later would give to him, (28:22).
31. She was Isaac's father's great niece, (ch 22:20-23).
35. Isaac _____ that Jacob was in fact Esau, (to 39A).
38. _____ promised to be with Jacob wherever he went.
39. (From 35A) because he recognized Jacob's _____, (to 23A) (27:22).
43. Rebekah wanted Jacob to go stay with her _____ in Padan-aram.
44. Raiment, or _____, (27:15, 27).[1]
45. (From 19D) ...and _____ his younger brother until...(to 46A).
46. (From 45A)... the _____ when he would break the yoke from upon his neck, (27:38-40).
48. Haran was the brother of _____, (ch 11:27; 28:2), (to 37D).
49. Isaac ate Jacob's tasty food and drank the _____.
50. Jacob's mother did as much scheming as her brother _____, (28:2; 29:21-30).
51. (From 26A) ...so that he could _____ the clothes his son was wearing, (27:26-27).
52. Rebekah planned the _____ of her husband for the sake of Jacob.

**Down:**
1. Esau was so hurt and angry about Jacob receiving his blessing, that he _____.
2. Isaac and Rebekah were not only husband and wife, they were also _____.
3. Jacob's blessing provided the enjoyment of the _____ of the earth, (to 47D).
4. Jacob left _____ and his family to go to Haran.
5. Isaac could not _____ the skin of a goat from the skin of his son Esau.
7. Because of his age, Isaac's eyes were _____.

(Continued next page; **Puzzle Grid on page 23**)

**Birthrights & Blessings (Down Continued):**

9.  (From 36D)  Esau sold his birthright willingly for a serving of red _____, (ch 25:29-34).

14.  Dreadful can also be described as _____, (28:17).[2]

16.  Part of Jacob's blessing was to be _____ over his brethren, (27:28-29).

18.  (From 24A)...with angels of God _____ and descending.

19.  Esau was destined to live by the _____, (to 45A), (27:38-40).

21.  _____ is translated as 'House of God', (28:17-22).[3]

22.  The stone pillar that Isaac anointed was called God's _____.

25.  God _____ with Rebekah and Jacob's deception of Isaac, (to 12A).

27.  To discern, understand, or _____, (27:23).[4]

29.  Puzzle content designed by _____ Johnson.

30.  Venison translates as _____ in this story, (27:3).[5]

32.  Isaac loved Esau's _____ meat, (27:9).

33.  (From 2A) ...but to choose a _____ of his Uncle Laban.

34.  When his twins were born, Isaac was _____ years old, (ch 25:26).

35.  Isaac blessed his sons when he thought that his _____ was not far off.

36.  Esau claimed that Jacob stole his _____, but, (to 9D).

37.  (From 48A)...therefore, Haran was Jacob's great _____.

40.  To mislead.

41.  Esau was _____ years old when he married his first wife, (ch 26:34).

42.  A young goat, (Merriam-Webster Dictionary).[6]

47.  (From 3D) ...including corn, wine, and the dew of _____.

50.  Jacob told his father the _____ brought the venison to him.

[1, 2, 3, 4, 5,] Wayne F. Brindle, et al. eds., *The King James Study Bible*, (Lynchburg, VA, Liberty University, 1988), pgs 55-59.

[6]    http://www.merriam-webster.com

# Birthrights & Blessings
## Genesis 27 – 28
### (KJV)

**(From Page 21: To find the correct place for each answer, read the numbers from left to right, line by line, horizontally, whether the clue is Across or Down.)**

## Jacob's Ancestry

**Seth** lived 105 years, when he begat Enos, Gen 5:6;
Enos lived 99 years, when he begat Cainan;
Cainan lived 70 years, when he begat Mahalaleel: Gen 5:12;
Mahalaleel lived 65 years, when he begat Jared, Gen 5:15;
Jared lived 162 years, when he begat **Enoch**, Gen 5:18.

Enoch lived 65 years, when he begat Methuselah, Gen 5:21; Enoch walked with God: [365 years] and he [was] not; for God took him, Gen 5:24. Methuselah lived 187 years, when he begat Lamech, Gen 5:25; all the days of Methuselah were 969 years: and he died, Gen 5:27. Lamech lived 182 years, when he begat a son, ([**Noah**], Gen 5:28-29.

Noah was 500 years old: and Noah begat **Shem**, Ham, and Japheth, Gen 5:32.

The children of **Shem**; Elam, and Asshur, and Arphaxad, and Lud, and Aram, Gen 10:22-29; And the children of Aram; Uz, and Hul, and Gether, and Mash; **Arphaxad** begat Salah; and Salah begat Eber; And **Joktan** begat Almodad, and Sheleph, and Hazarmaveth, and Jerah; and Hadoram, and Uzal, and Diklah; and Obal, and Abimael, and Sheba; and Ophir, and Havilah, and Jobab: all these [were] the sons of Joktan.

**Shem** [was] 100 years old, when he begat **Arphaxad** two years after the flood, Gen 11:10; and Arphaxad lived 35 years, when he begat Salah, Gen 11:12. Salah lived 30 years, when he begat Eber, Gen 11:14; And Eber lived 34 years, when he begat **Peleg**, Gen 11:16.

**Peleg** lived thirty years, when he begat Reu, Gen 11:18;
Reu lived 32 years, when he begat **Serug**, Gen 11:20;
Serug lived 30 years, when he begat **Nahor**, Gen 11:22;
Nahor lived 29 years, when he begat **Terah**;
**Terah** lived 70 years, when he begat **Abram**, Nahor, and Haran, Gen 11:26.
And Terah begat Abram, Nahor, and Haran; and Haran begat Lot, Gen 11:27.

Hagar [Sarai's handmaiden] bare Abram a son: and Abram [at 86 years old] called his son's name, which Hagar bare, Ishmael; Gen 16:15; 17:24-25.

**Abraham** was 100 years old, when his son **Isaac** was born unto him, Gen 21:5.

And the LORD said unto her [Rebekah], Two nations [are] in thy womb, and two manner of people shall be separated from thy bowels; and [the one] people shall be stronger than [the other] people; and the elder shall serve the younger; …behold, [there were] twins in her womb; And the first came out red, all over like an hairy garment; and they called his name Esau; And after that came his brother out, and his hand took hold on **Esau's** heel; and his name was called **Jacob**: and Isaac [was] 60 years old when she [Rebekah] bare them, Genesis 25:23-26.

## A Bride For Jacob

---

Even before he was to marry,
Isaac and Rebekah worried
That Jacob (nor Esau) marry a daughter of Canaan.


And Rebekah said to Isaac, 'I am weary
because of the daughters of Heth:
If Jacob takes a wife of their daughters
such as the daughters of the land, [of Canaan]
What good shall my life do me?'
(from Gen 27:46)


And Isaac called Jacob, and blessed him,
and charged him, and said unto him,
'Thou shall not take a wife
of the daughters of Canaan.


'Prepare to go to Padanaram,
to the house of Bethuel, thy mother's father;
and take yourself a wife
from the daughters of Laban,
thy mother's brother.'
(Gen 28:1-2)


So Jacob went in search of
his mother's family…
And he came upon a well in the land of Haran
and found Rachel there…
She came to give water to her father's sheep:
Now, Laban had two daughters…
Leah, the eldest, and… Rachel, the youngest,
And Jacob loved Rachel…
(from Gen 29:9, 16, 18)

## Jacob Chooses A Bride
### Genesis 29-30,
### (KVJ)

Words are found below that represent answers to clues listed on the next page. Figure out the answers and circle them in the grid. You may find words that are not intended as part of the lesson puzzle; it's all good. Words can go across, left to right; down, and in any diagonal. Some words may appear more than once.

```
L  K  P  D  W  B  G  L  K  G  Z  Y  V  H  V  T  H  I  R  D
Z  X  B  I  A  V  K  I  L  R  Q  R  M  O  N  T  H  C  Q  N
R  T  V  R  F  Y  S  C  S  A  V  M  V  C  T  M  N  M  R  L
H  E  R  N  T  S  B  I  X  N  B  I  L  H  A  H  Y  X  G  D
S  E  U  I  E  D  M  N  X  D  N  T  G  V  L  R  L  T  E  E
N  Z  N  D  C  E  H  R  R  S  E  J  U  D  A  H  F  L  N  C
R  K  L  R  O  K  V  T  D  O  G  C  F  G  W  E  L  L  E  E
A  M  O  N  K  R  E  E  M  N  J  N  E  H  K  X  N  V  S  I
C  N  V  X  B  N  V  D  M  H  I  G  H  P  Y  B  I  T  I  V
H  N  E  F  A  O  Q  C  S  N  F  M  T  Q  T  T  R  E  S  E
E  G  D  R  L  I  L  D  G  I  N  W  V  D  A  I  S  N  W  K
L  R  A  X  V  O  M  W  R  X  S  L  O  L  Y  H  V  D  B  P
Z  H  B  E  M  T  C  S  Y  R  W  T  E  M  E  N  N  E  T  R
I  L  L  N  Y  F  T  K  B  T  L  R  E  E  B  L  A  R  D  E
L  P  Q  X  K  B  O  O  R  D  H  P  P  R  X  U  M  N  Y  U
P  T  T  E  O  K  C  U  C  L  Y  R  Z  L  T  V  O  F  R  B
A  Y  E  R  W  A  J  M  R  K  L  X  E  I  Z  C  I  P  O  E
H  W  N  M  J  Q  P  Z  G  T  R  G  F  E  E  R  S  W  L  N
L  T  J  J  O  H  N  S  O  N  H  U  T  S  S  K  T  O  M  N
H  F  O  U  R  T  E  E  N  T  L  Z  T  T  N  H  V  V  N  T
```

**Jacob Chooses A Bride…Clues:**
**(For proper Hebrew translation, look up names of Jacob's sons)**

Rachel had no children, she was _____

Jacob served Laban _____ years for Rachel and Leah

Jacob moved a stone from a well for _____

Judah was the _____ born son

To beguile is to _____


Rachel was a _____ woman

His name literally translates as 'Praise' [1]

Jacob stayed with Laban a _____ before negotiating for a wife

Brother can mean _____

Rachel kept her father's _____


A younger daughter could not marry _____

Reuben was Jacob's _____ son (2 words)

In this story, son of Nahor refers to the _____ of Nahor

His name translates as 'Heard' [3]

Jacob _____ Rachel


Literal translation of _____ is 'son' [2]

Puzzle content by _____

All the _____ must be gathered before any of them could drink

Simeon was the _____ born son

Leah was _____ eyed


Jacob's mother was Laban's _____

Levi was the _____ born son

God gave Leah a _____ first because she was unloved

The wedding feast lasted a _____

Laban had _____ daughters


Jacob was paid in _____ versus money

Jacob met some men near a _____ in Haran

Land of people of the east, in this story, meant near _____

'Hated' in verse 31 means ____ [4]

She was Rachel's handmaiden


Jacob _____ Rachel when he first met her

His name literally means 'Attached' [5]

He commanded action of men he didn't know (v7)

Laban _____ Jacob by giving him Leah instead of Rachel

There were _____ flocks of sheep waiting to drink when Jacob approached the well.

Laban was _____ like Jacob

God finally opened Rachel's _____

Puzzle story from _____, ch 29-30

1, 2, 3, 4, 5,     http://www.blueletterbible.org

27

**Jacob's Family**,
**Genesis 29:31-35; Chapter 30**,
**(KJV)**

The characters below form answers to the clues listed on the following page. Figure out what words the clues represent and circle them in the grid. Words can go across, left to right; up and down, and in three diagonals. You may find a few unscripted words in the grid. And words may appear more than once.

```
T  F  H  T  T  T  U  N  L  O  V  E  D  M  T  Y
R  A  C  H  E  L  M  P  L  H  T  V  P  R  J  R
Y  J  M  P  W  M  R  A  A  N  T  Z  A  G  J  N
N  Z  I  L  P  A  H  D  N  M  M  H  P  M  O  B
B  W  H  K  L  C  U  R  H  D  C  C  I  Q  H  E
I  L  T  L  E  J  N  A  N  A  R  L  R  K  N  N
B  E  C  A  V  Q  N  E  S  J  A  A  D  M  S  J
L  A  B  B  I  I  B  S  T  T  A  N  K  L  O  A
E  H  C  A  D  U  I  S  H  R  I  C  K  E  N  M
G  T  L  N  E  D  U  P  I  Z  I  S  O  C  S  I
R  A  F  R  O  A  A  K  I  M  E  B  S  B  K  N
T  A  D  G  S  N  K  Q  C  S  E  B  E  A  D  N
P  S  D  E  J  O  S  E  P  H  R  O  U  S  C  L
C  H  A  R  E  B  E  K  A  H  K  A  N  L  P  Y
H  E  N  K  Y  B  I  L  H  A  H  N  E  Z  U  N
V  R  J  U  D  G  E  M  E  N  T  V  N  L  F  N
```

**Jacob's Family...Clues:**
**(For proper Hebrew translation, look up names of Jacob's sons)**

Name means 'Happy' [1]

Mother of Dan & Naphtali' [2]

Only girl in genealogy of Jacob's children

This puzzle is a _____ study

Name means 'Judge' [3]

Jacob's twin brother

Name means 'Troop' or 'Fortune' [4]

Jacob's Spiritual name

Name means 'Reward' or 'Hire' [5]

He renamed Jacob

Jacob's father

Husband of four wives

Name means 'He will add' [6]

Meaning of Dinah's name [8]

Mother of Dinah

Name means 'Praise' [7]

Jacob's father-in-law

Jacob's mother

Name means 'Attached' [9]

Name means 'Wrestling' [10]

The wife Jacob truly loved

Herb with small yellow fruit

Hated in Ch 29:31 [11]

Jacob's firstborn son

His name means 'Heard' [12]

Jacob's sons later called _____ of Israel

Name means 'Dwelling' [13]

Son of Jacob's old age

Mother of Asher and Gad

Puzzle author

[1-13] http://www.blueletterbible.org

**Trickery Among Men,**
**For Sheep & Goats**
**Genesis 30:25 - 43,**
**(KJV)**

These characters include answers to clues found on the following page. Find and circle the answers in the grid. Words can go across, up and down, left to right, and in three diagonals. Unscripted words may be found in the puzzle as well, and words may appear more than once..

```
H  B  N  T  L  H  J  N  P  E  E  L  E  D  P  L  F  T
N  X  M  K  R  R  I  P  M  L  L  W  L  T  Q  W  E  H
M  K  R  N  T  O  O  R  L  A  N  K  E  R  E  X  E  R
C  A  T  T  L  E  U  D  E  B  X  R  R  A  X  N  B  E
B  Q  W  L  C  Z  P  G  S  A  G  N  P  V  L  M  L  E
J  H  O  U  S  E  L  N  H  N  Q  Z  M  H  N  T  E  D
S  A  X  L  Q  K  Z  K  R  S  R  K  L  O  N  D  H  C
L  T  C  C  O  N  C  E  I  V  E  K  S  L  E  D  K  Y
I  U  R  O  B  E  T  W  E  E  N  N  J  R  N  K  T  C
V  N  X  O  B  X  G  F  R  R  H  N  E  W  T  E  S  X
E  H  T  H  N  X  L  T  H  O  Q  P  O  U  M  Z  H  C
S  A  T  S  N  G  Y  B  J  N  S  R  N  A  Y  J  E  P
T  P  H  H  T  T  R  J  E  O  B  T  N  G  C  T  E  R
O  P  X  E  Y  E  T  E  R  F  S  Y  L  G  T  Z  P  Y
C  Y  W  B  H  R  R  P  V  E  A  R  M  F  O  T  L  D
K  T  L  T  V  G  J  P  H  T  B  F  N  P  L  A  G  C
B  K  A  B  D  N  P  C  S  C  O  U  N  T  R  Y  T  T
G  F  Q  Y  T  P  T  C  S  T  R  E  A  K  E  D  H  S
```

**Trickery Among Men...Clues:**
**(Ch is used for Chapter of same book; V is used for Verse of puzzle reference chapter)**

Betwixt, same as _____

Jacob took all the speckled, spotted, and _____ cattle as his own

Livestock called _____, or sheep

Jacob used rods of Hazel and _____ trees to help him captivate the flock

The rods helped the flock to _____


Jacob longed to return to his _____

Laban was Jacob's _____ -in-law

The unspotted and _____ cattle belonged to Laban

The he- _____ were ring-streaked

Jacob also used rods of _____ poplar in his livestock repopulation system


Wages or _____

Jacob wanted to provide for his own _____

God blessed Laban because of _____

Father of Rachel and Leah

Jacob chose _____ as his wages in this story


To appoint is to _____

Also spelled 'pilled' in this story

Increased exceedingly

These had strange power over the cattle Jacob tended

The ___ -goats were speckled or spotted


Cattle in this story are really _____

To tarry

Ring streaked or _____

The spotted and _____ cattle belonged to Jacob, (V 42)

Laban changed Jacob's pay _____ times (Ch 31:7)


_____ days passed before Laban knew Jacob had departed his camp (Ch 31:32)

Rods were placed in the watering _____ to help the flock conceive

Laban was most _____ with the results of Jacob's experimentation

Puzzle content by _____

Jacob became very _____ while serving Laban.

## Jacob Leaves Laban
## Genesis 31 – 32, (KJV)

**Across:**

1. He told Jacob to return to his kindred.
5. After Jacob left Laban, it took Laban _____ days before he caught up with him.
6. Jegar-sahadutha is the _____ version of 'The Heap of Witness'. [1]
8. Covenant in verse 44 means _____. [2]
10. Land of Bethuel and Laban.
12. When Jacob's name was changed; he said, "I have seen God face to _____," (to 28D)
13. Altogether, Jacob worked for Laban _____ years.
14. The brook Jabbok is called a _____ in chapter 32:22.
16. Nahor was great grandfather of Rachel and _____. [3]
17. The Lord _____ between me & thee....
18. (from 11D) ...nor would they pass beyond the stone _____ Jacob built to harm the other.
19. God warned Laban to speak neither _____ nor bad of Jacob.
25. Sons of 31:28 refer to _____.
27. The heap of stones served as a _____ to the agreement between Jacob and Laban.
29. To rebuke is translated as _____. [4]
30. Rachel and Leah were _____.
31. Rachel stole the images that belonged to her _____.
32. Jacob's brother Esau lived in the country of _____.
33. Synonymous with transgression. [5]
37. Suffered in 31:28 translates as _____. [6]
38. _____ charged Jacob not to marry other wives.
39. Nahor was Laban and Rebekah's _____. [7]
43. Wroth in 31:36 can be translated as _____. [8]
45. Nahor was Jacob's great _____. [9]
47. The angel of God told Jacob to return to his _____.
49. Peradventure. [10]
51. Jacob and his wives left Laban's camp without saying _____.
53. Puzzle content designed by tj _____.
54. To discern or _____. [11]
55. Jacob told Laban he left secretly because he didn't want to lose his _____.
56. Furniture of 31:34 refers to _____. [12]

**Down:**

1. Jacob and family were camped in Mount _____ when Laban found them.
2. Today's state or country of the Jewish people is _____.
3. Cows in these verses are referred to as _____.
4. Mirth can be defined as _____. [13]
7. She stole her father's household idol.
8. Same as tabret. [14]

(Clues continued on page 35)

## Jacob Leaves Laban
## Genesis 31 – 32, (KJV)

**(Note: Puzzle numbers read from left to right, line by line, horizontally)**

## Jacob Returns To His Country
## And His Kindred


...And Jacob was extremely concerned

About seeing his brother again;

Even though the LORD told Jacob

To return to his country

And his people.



When Jacob had last seen his brother,

Esau had promised to kill Jacob, after

Their father Isaac died.



Now, it is time..., some

Twenty years later,

And Jacob makes preparations

To face Esau,

Again.



So, Jacob divided his caravan

Into two companies...

And he sent messengers

Before him to meet Esau,

Along with many, many gifts.


(Genesis 27:41; 31:11-14, 38; 32:3, 7-9; 18)

## Jacob Leaves Laban (Down: Continued from page 32):

9.  Laban searched all their _____, but did not find the images.
10.  The name 'Israel' translates as '_____ with God'. [15]
11.  A condition of covenant between Laban and Jacob: Jacob would not _____ Laban's daughters, (to 18A).
15.  As they traveled, Jacob divided his people and possessions into _____.
19.  A female _____ is called a kid. [16]
20.  Nahor was his brother. [17]
21.  The stories of this chapter happened before Jacob's youngest _____ was born.
22.  Jacob vowed _____ to whoever had taken Laban's idol gods.
23.  Gen 32:22 says Jacob had _____ wives.
24.  Ram is a male _____. [18]
26.  Laban was of _____ ancestry.
28.  (from 12A)...."and my life is _____," (Gen 32:30).
29.  Rachel hid her father's images in the _____ furniture.
31.  A ewe is a _____ sheep. [19]
34.  Jacob built a pillar of _____.
35.  Jacob believed that he had wrestled with _____.
36.  Abram's father's father was named _____, (Gen 11:24-26).
39.  Hebrew for 'The Heap of Witness'. [20]
40.  Jacob gladly worked _____ years for his wives.
41.  Rachel is _____ word for ewe. [21]
42.  Word for watch over, or watch between. [22]
43.  Words in 'Italics' have been _____ to Scripture for clarity.
44.  Gray-spotted, or _____. [23]
46.  God of Abraham, and the God of _____, (31:53).
48.  God called Himself the God of _____, (31:13).
50.  Called images in the Scripture. [24]
52.  Breeding the livestock cost Jacob _____ years.

[1-15, 17, 20, 22-24] Wayne A. Brindle, et al, eds., *The King James Study Bible,* (Lynchburg, VA: Liberty University, 1988).

[16, 19, 21] http://www.blueletterbible.org

[18] http://www.merriweather-webster.com

## Meeting Esau Again
### Genesis 32-33, (KJV)

**Across:**

1. Jacob sent _____ to his brother Esau.
8. Used to describe a flock or herd, (ch 32). [1]
9. Host, as in verse 2. [2]
10. El-elohe-Israel translates as _____, The God of Israel. [3]
11. Jacob's thigh shrank when _____ touched it.
12. The name Israel literally means _____ with God.
14. Esau ran to meet Jacob and _____ him.
17. Jacob's wrestling match took place at the ford _____.
18. Meaning of Mahanaim. (2 wds) [4]
22. At the time of this story, Jacob had _____ sons.
23. Jacob built another _____ at Shalem, a city of Shechem in Canaan, (33:18-20).
27. When Jacob first crossed the Jordan, he had only his _____ to support him.
29. Jacob wrestled with the angel to get a _____.
31. Same as halted. [5]
33. Seed can be described as one's _____, (pl). [6]
34. Alternate spelling for Peniel. [7]
36. Jacob and Esau kissed each other and _____.
37. Succoth got its name from the _____ that Jacob built. [8]
40. Esau lived in this place.
42. Bilhah and Zilpah are called _____ in chapter 32, (2 wds (?)).
43. Puzzle content created by _____.
44. Muscle. [9]

**Down:**

2. Jacob bowed to the ground _____ times after crossing the Jabbok River.
3. Verse 22 speaks of Jacob's _____ wives.
4. He was the last person to leave the camp of Peniel.
5. Used synonymously with thigh. [10]
6. Jacob _____ Esau to accept his gifts.
7. The _____ of Jacob's thigh or hip is also defined as the socket. [11]
12. Word for 'Face of God' _____. [12]
13. The state of _____ established on May 15, 1948, (Hint: of Jacob).
15. The bands Jacob arranged interpret as _____. [13]
16. Another word for grace. [14]
19. Mercies translate as _____, (2 wds). [15]
20. _____ of Israel don't eat the muscle of the thigh because of Jacob's injured thigh.
21. Jacob sent _____ to test Esau's mood, (pl).
24. Jacob was _____ when he heard of Esau's men.
25. Jacob's thigh was out of _____, (32;35).
26. Womenservants, maidservants, and _____ are the same, (Could be 2 wds).
28. This word means to pass over, (v 22). [16]
30. Seir interpreted as shaggy or _____. [17]
32. Shalem also spelled Salem, meaning _____. [18]
(Continued, bottom of puzzle grid)

# Meeting Esau Again, Genesis 32-33, (KJV)

**(Read numbers from left to right, line by line, to find correct spaces for answers)**

35. Drove in chapter 33:8 refers to _____. [19]
37. Jacob divided his family and servants into two _____.
38. One verse calls the Jabbok a ford, one verse calls it a _____.
39. With _____ hundred men, Esau traveled to meet Jacob.
41. Jacob wrestled with a _____ till dawn.

[1, 16-18]     http://www.blueletterbible.org
[2-15, 19]        Wayne A. Brindle, et al. eds., *The King James Study Bible,* (Lynchburg, VA: Liberty University, 1988).

## Dinah's Dilemma,
## Genesis 34-35, (KJV)

**Across:**

1. Bethel translates as 'House of _____ ". [1]
4. Hamor proposed that Jacob's family _____ with his family.
8. God told Jacob to go up to _____ and build an altar.
10. Simeon and Levi took _____ out of Shechem's house after their murderous rampage.
12. Hamar's family were _____ by heritage, (plural).
13. He called his new son, 'Son of my right hand.' [2]
16. Original name of Bethel. [3]
17. Two of Dinah's brothers murdered all the men of Hamor to vindicate their sister's _____.
18. God promised Jacob the _____ of Abraham and Isaac.
21. Strange can also be described as _____. [4]
24. Jacob instructed his household to put away their _____ gods.
26. Dinah had _____ brothers.
28. Seat of virility, hips, or thigh refers to the term _____, (always plural in Bible). [5]
29. After he had dishonored Jacob's daughter, Shechem asked Jacob to show him _____.
31. According to verse 19, Shechem was more _____ than all his father's house.
33. (from 35D) …they did not want Dinah to _____ Shechem.
34. The name of the place in this story where Jacob built an altar was _____.
36. Jacob told his people to _____ themselves before going to Bethel. [6]
37. Violated or _____. [7]
38. Dinah's brothers _____ all the property of Shechem's city.

**Down:**

2. By lying with Dinah, Shechem did a_____ thing.
3. Hamor had his eyes on Jacob's cattle & other _____.
5. God told Israel to be fruitful and _____, (to 14D).
6. _____ of Dinah's brothers had the same mother as Dinah.
7. Son of my sorrow is the translation for _____. [8]
9. Without _____, Shechem agreed to the request of Jacob's sons.
11. Shechem's father was _____, the Hivite.
12. Jacob's sons demanded _____ of Hamor's men in order for Shechem to marry Dinah.
13. He was very upset with Simeon and Levi's actions.
14. (from 5D) and _____ shall come from your loins.
15. Puzzle content by tj _____.
19. Dinah longed for _____ companionship, according to 34:1.
20. Rachel died giving birth to _____.
22. In Ch 35:10, God again tells Jacob his new _____.
23. An oak tree is also called a _____ tree. [9]
25. His name was also the name of a town in Canaan.
27. Fear of the _____ of God prevented anyone from pursuing Jacob's family when they left Hamor's land.
30. Jacob poured a drink offering and an _____ offering on the pillar of stone.
32. Shechem's father was called _____ of the country.
35. Jacob's sons planned to _____ Hamar and Shechem; because (to 33A)

# Dinah's Dilemma, Genesis 34-35
## (KJV)

**(Numbers read from left to right, line by line, horizontally, to find correct answer spaces)**

[1, 5] http://www.blueletterbible.org

[2, 3,4, 6-9] Wayne A. Brindle et. al. eds., *The King James Study Bible,* (Lynchburg, VA: Liberty University, 1988), pp. 69-72.

## The Dreamer, Genesis 37:1-11, (KJV)

**Across:**
3. Joseph's second dream included eleven _____, as did the first dream.
6. The same is Jacob.
9. Naphtali and _____ were the sons of Bilhah. (v2; Gen 35:25).
10. Joseph's brothers did not want him to have _____ over them.
11. Joseph said, "...behold your sheaves stood round about _____."
14. When Jacob heard about these dreams he _____ Joseph.
16. Joseph reported _____ news to his father about his brothers.
17. Sheaves can be translated as _____. [1]
18. The land where Jacob's forefathers had dwelled.
20. Generation (v2) can be interpreted as _____. [2]
21. Joseph was _____ years old in this story.
22. She was Rachel's older sister.
26. To make obeisance is the same as to _____ down.
27. Heavenly bodies bowed _____ to Joseph in a dream.
28. Jacob _____ Joseph more than his other sons, (from 1D).
33. Jacob truly loved only _____ woman.
34. The family of Jacob had been _____ in that land for many years.
38. Joseph dreamed again, yet _____ dream.
40. Joseph fed his father's _____ as did his older brothers.
42. Stars in his dream, and Joseph's brothers, equal the same number: _____.
43. When Joseph talked of his dreams, his brothers hated him _____.
44. Sheaves refer to bundled or _____ things. [3]

**Down:**
1. Joseph's brothers _____ him not only because of his dreams, but also because..., (to 28A).
2. Brothers, as used in this puzzle, refer to Joseph's _____ brothers.
3. The second dream included the _____ and the moon.
4. Rebuke means to _____.
5. Jacob's sons would become known as the _____ of Israel.
7. The older boys could not _____ in a peaceful manner to Joseph.
8. A temporary resident in Bible times.
11. Joseph's father kept the _____ of Joseph's dreams in his mind.
12. Joseph's mother.
13. To have dominion is to _____, (to 19D)
15. Joseph's younger brother.
19. (From 13D) ... _____, as a king or ruler.
21. In his first dream, Joseph dreamed about _____.
23. The number _____ is a significant number in the Bible.
24. (From 31D) ...Jacob said, "Shall I and thy _____ bow down to you?"
25. Joseph's coat had many _____.
29. This puzzle content was created by tj _____.
30. Grandfather to Jacob's sons.

(Continued on next page, bottom of puzzle grid)

## The Dreamer,
## Genesis 37:1-11, (KJV)

**(To find the correct spaces for each answer, read the numbers from left to right, line by line, horizontally, regardless of whether the clue is Across or Down.)**

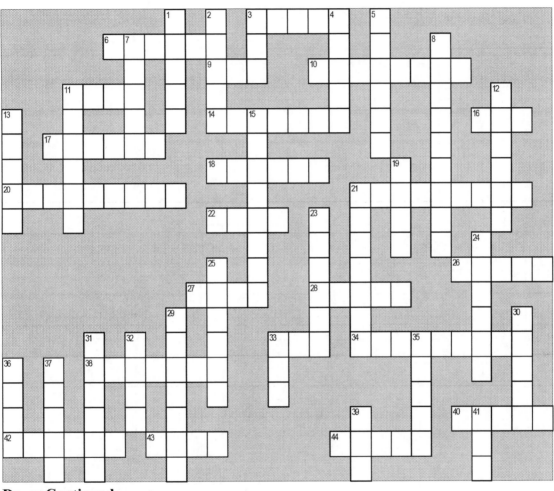

## Down Continued:

31. When Joseph told his _____ about his dream, (to 24D).
32. _____ women gave birth to the sons of Jacob.
33. Benjamin was the son of his father's _____ age.
34. Italics in scripture indicate that the word was _____ for clarity.

_(35. Italics in scripture indicate that the word was _____ for clarity.)_

35. Italics in scripture indicate that the word was _____ for clarity.
36. Same as dwell.
37. Gad and _____ were sons of Zilpah, (v2; Gen 35:26).
39. The _____ of Abraham, Isaac, and Jacob.
41. In this story, Joseph is referred to as a _____.

1  http://www.blueletterbible.org
2  http://www.merriam-webster.com
3  http://www.blueletterbible.org

## Plot To Kill Joseph
### Genesis 37:11-36, (KJV)

**(Read numbers from left to right, line by line, to find correct spaces for answers)**

**(Note: Ch is used for Chapter of same book; V is used for Verse of puzzle chapter)**

**Across:**

5. They, Joseph's brothers, brought Joseph's blood-stained coat to their _____.
7. A caravan of _____ came by carrying goods to Egypt.
9. Jacob fathered _____ sons by his wife Rachel, (ch 35:23-26).
10. Rueben was the _____ of Jacob's sons.
12. Jacob _____ his clothes and mourned for Joseph upon hearing what his sons told him.
13. Joseph found his brothers minding the flock in _____.
15. Joseph's _____, also called a coat.

(Continued next page)

**Plot To Kill Joseph,**
**(Across: Continued):**

16. She was Leah's handmaiden, (ch 35:26)
19. There was no _____ in the pit where Joseph was thrown.
20. A _____ man told Joseph where to find his brothers tending sheep.
21. Joseph was sold for _____ pieces of silver.
24. Israel sent Joseph to keep an _____ on his brothers.
25. Jacob placed a _____ on Rachel's grave, (ch 35:19-20).
28. Egypt lay _____ of where thy fed their flock.
29. The animal they killed is the same as a_____ goat.
30. His brothers planned to throw Joseph in a _____.
32. Leah gave birth to _____ sons, (ch 35:23).
33. At first, Joseph's brothers planned to _____ him.
34. This puzzle content designed by _____ johnson.
35. Word often used to indicate brothers.
37. The conspirators told their father they had _____ Joseph's coat.
39. Joseph's brothers wanted to avoid _____ his blood.
41. An early name of Bethlehem, (ch 35:19).
42. A _____ can be cattle, sheep, or goats.
45. Child, as used in this passage means _____.
46. Dreamer, as used in verse nineteen, refers to lord or _____ of dreams. [1]

**Down**:

1. Joseph was to bring his father _____ about his brothers.
2. _____ believed that an evil beast had torn Joseph into pieces.
3. Rachel died during _____, (ch 35:16-19).
4. After disposing of Joseph, his brothers sat down to _____.
6. It was his idea to sell Joseph to the Ishmaelites.
8. In verse 12, the flock was feeding in _____.
11. A caravan carried _____ as part of their payload.
14. Ishmaelites, used synonymously to mean _____, (v 27-28).
17. Bilhah was handmaiden to _____, (ch 35:23-26).
18. Reuben returned to the pit and found Joseph _____.
22. You could say that Joseph's brothers _____ him and his dreams.
23. When Joseph found his brothers in Dothan, they were very _____ with him.
26. _____ convinced the others not to kill Joseph.
27. Jacob and his family were camped in the vale of _____.
30. The merchants sold Joseph to an officer of Pharaoh's court named _____, (ch 39:1).
31. A likely alibi was to tell Jacob that a wild _____ devoured Joseph.
36. Joseph wandered about in a _____ in Shechem before he found his brothers.
38. Joseph was accused of being a _____.
40. The merchant travelers took Joseph to _____.
43. To slay is the same as to _____.
44. A _____ goat was slain to get blood to put on Joseph's coat.

---

[1]    46D    http://www.blueletterbible.org

## Sons of Judah
## Genesis 38, (KJV)

**Across**:

1. According to Mosaic _____, one brother must marry his dead brother's wife to father a child, (if the dead brother had no children), (Deut 25:5-6).
3. Judah's three sons were all to marry the same _____.
8. This puzzle content created by tj _____
10. Zerah translates as _____, (see Bible Dictionary). [1]
11. Afraid for Shelah's _____, Judah promised him to Tamar, after he had grown up.
12. Judah's father.
14. The newborn with the scarlet _____ on his hand was actually born last.
18. Christ, the Son of God, is the _____.
21. Christ is further translated as the _____. [2]
27. Tamar asked for a _____ before consenting to Judah's proposal.
29. Judah wanted to _____Tamar when he was told she was with child.
30. After three _____ Judah found that his daughter-in-law had fooled him.
31. Judah declared that Tamar had been more _____ than he had.
34. Judah fathered _____ born to his daughter-in-law.
35. Mother of Judah.
37. Translation of Pharez is _____ or Breakthrough. [3]
38. Tamar bargained for _____ things from Judah as a promise to keep his word.
39. The LORD _____ Er.
41. An ancestor of Jesus, born from the union of Judah and Tamar.
42. The third son of Judah.
43. Judah left his brothers and went down toward _____.
45. A short word that gives options.
46. _____ is sometimes spelled Zerah.
49. Tamar went to live in her father's _____ after the death of her second husband.
50. Judah offered his _____, along with other things as a guarantee of his word.
51. Judah thought the woman he met by the roadside was a _____.
52. In total, Judah fathered _____ sons, (Gen 46:12).

**Down**:

1. Christ is described as the _____ of the tribe of Judah, (Rev. 5:5)
2. The LORD considered Er to be wicked or _____.
4. The term 'took her' means that he _____ her.
5. Judah was not the first born of Jacob, but the _____, (Gen 29:35).
6. Simple sentence or thought connector.
7. In later years, Judah became a _____ among his brothers.
9. Shelah translates as _____. [4]
13. A Canaanite is one who is a descendant of _____.
15. The oldest of Judah's sons.

(Continued on page 47)

## Sons of Judah,
## Genesis 38, (KJV)

**(Numbers read from left to right, line by line, horizontally, for correct answer spaces)**

(Clues continued on page 47)

## Judah and Tamar

---

When Tamar's second husband died,
She went back to her father's house
to wait for Shelah to grow up
...and marry her,
As Judah had promised.


Shelah matured, but Judah
reneged...on his pledge, so...
Tamar was set on
Reckoning...
The matter.


When she heard that Judah
was visiting nearby,
She discarded her widow's garments
and dressed to hide her
Identity.
Judah thought her to be
a harlot, seeing her sitting
Beside the road.


And so...
he bargained with her
on her price...
As a result, she was with child
in fact more than one...
Twins were born to her of
Judah... namely,
Pharez and Zarah.


(from Genesis 38)

**Sons of Judah,
Genesis 38, (KJV)**

**(Down: Continued from page 44):**

16. Judah married the _____ of a Canaanite.
17. The LORD 'slew' him means he _____ him.
19. A pledge is _____ given to seal a promise.
20. When Shelah did not marry her, Tamar was _____.
22. Tamar shed her widow's _____ and sat by the side of the road, waiting for Judah.
23. Tamar was a _____ and pregnant.
24. The thing which Onan did _____ the LORD.
25. Christ is a descendant of the tribe of _____.
26. Judah's second son.
28. Shelah was the _____ son of Judah and his Canaanite wife.
32. The name of Er's wife.
33. An Adullamite who put Judah up for the night.
36. To 'turn in' might translate as 'to _____ a tent'. [5]
37. Er was Judah's first _____.
38. The name of Onan's wife.
40. Judah had _____ brothers.
41. Judah did not keep his _____ for Shelah to marry Tamar.
42. Judah's father-in-law, (v2, v12).
44. Judah translates as praise or _____, (past tense). [6]
47. Er was wicked in the sight of the _____.
48. Onan was _____ to father a child by his brother's widow.

[1] 10A   http://www.blueletterbible.org
[2] 21A   Merrill F. Unger, *Unger's Bible Dictionary*, Third Edition (Chicago: Moody Press, 1966) p. 195
[3] 37A   http://www.blueletterbible.org
[4] 9D   ibid
[5] 36D   ibid
[6] 44D   ibid

## Judah and Tamar,
## Genesis 38
## (KJV)

The clues on the following page represent answers found in the puzzle.  Words can read from left to right across, straight up and down, and in any diagonal.  Words can cross and share one letter.  You may also find unscripted words in the grid, and some words that appear more than once.

```
E  K  S  Z  R  J  L  H  R  H  I  R  A  H  L  L  F  T
L  R  E  T  J  J  O  H  N  S  O  N  T  V  K  K  R  D
E  T  C  K  B  P  F  E  R  Q  Q  O  H  T  L  E  A  H
V  Q  U  K  X  X  M  T  R  G  L  A  W  Q  T  H  V  P
E  P  R  V  H  A  E  R  R  U  I  J  R  F  W  K  R
N  W  I  P  R  L  O  M  A  H  N  V  A  P  H  M  H  I
D  N  T  R  C  T  K  H  S  S  P  C  C  K  D  R  T  G
X  W  Y  A  S  T  D  C  N  Y  H  T  O  R  P  K  K  H
P  L  R  E  T  K  T  W  L  E  S  Z  B  L  K  D  T  T
Z  B  C  X  L  W  D  A  L  B  E  C  E  K  H  I  R  E
C  N  C  A  Z  F  E  N  M  R  L  D  A  Q  D  S  D  O
A  O  S  Z  O  B  H  L  A  A  G  P  D  R  K  P  M  U
K  T  V  U  D  A  Y  H  V  E  R  X  G  T  L  L  F  S
T  L  R  E  D  T  P  Q  K  E  B  R  O  T  H  E  R  S
W  T  Z  U  R  C  A  N  A  A  N  J  P  W  C  A  T  D
H  R  J  Q  P  E  T  Y  R  R  G  N  M  O  Z  S  N  N
W  X  M  L  L  R  D  H  H  L  Q  P  K  R  V  E  L  P
R  X  N  M  Z  A  R  A  H  C  J  B  M  D  Q  D  N  V
```

**Clues for Judah and Sons, Word Search, previous page:**
**Genesis 38, KJV**

Pharez was an _____ of Jesus

Tamar was married to two _____

Tamar hid her _____ to conceal her identity

Judah had these many brothers

One gift Judah gave Tamar: _____

Judah's wife was a native of _____

Onan caused God to be _____

Firstborn of Judah, _____

Judah was the _____ son of Jacob

Adullamite friend of Judah

Christ was of the tribe of _____

Twin with thread on hand; born _____

Tamar was mistaken as a _____

Father of Judah

A young goat

Mother of Judah in Gen 29:35

The term 'took her' means to _____

The 'harlot' asked gifts as a _____

Tamar was more _____ than Judah

A _____ thread tied to a twins' hand

Meaning Breach or Breakthrough [1]

Judah's aunt: _____

Father-in-law of Judah

She was widowed twice

Gifts or pledges were given as _____

Puzzle content creator

Of _____ sons, Judah would emerge as a forefather of Jesus

Judah fathered _____ by Tamar

Judah did not keep his _____

Also spelled as 'Zerah'

---

[1] http://www.blueletterbible.org

**In Potiphar's House, Genesis 39, (KJV)**

**(Read the numbers from left to right, line by line, horizontally, for Across or Down clues.)**

**Across:**
1. The merchants who took Joseph to Egypt were relatives of _____.
3. Whatever Joseph attempted to do, he did _____.
6. Joseph found _____ in God's sight.
7. Potiphar became _____ when he heard his wife's story.
10. Everything Joseph did _____.
13. The prison keeper _____ everything to Joseph's care.
16. Anything in Joseph's care was blessed, including the house, and the planted _____.
17. The chief warden put Joseph in _____ of all the prisoners where he was jailed.
19. Joseph refused to _____ against God.
21. Joseph's brothers had no _____ where Joseph would end up when they sold him.

(Continued next page)

## In Potiphar's House (Across: Continued):
22. Potiphar's wife convinced her husband that Joseph made a _____ at her.
24. The LORD blessed Potiphar's house because of _____.
26. This crossword is designed to _____ you study the Bible.
27. To mock is to _____ at. [1]
30. Potiphar's wife _____ him for bringing Joseph to their house.
31. When Mrs. Potiphar made advances toward Joseph he _____.
33. Joseph was a most _____ man.
34. _____ wrote the book of Genesis.
36. The LORD was _____ Joseph.
40. Joseph left part of his _____ behind as he ran to escape Mrs. Potiphar.
42. Mrs. Potiphar said she cried with a _____ voice because of Joseph's advances.
43. The LORD God _____ Joseph because Joseph blessed God.
45. (From 46A)…and _____ to everyone about what had happened.
46. Mrs. Potiphar invented a convincing _____ about Joseph, (to 45A).
48. Joseph was put in jail with the _____ prisoners.
49. Joseph was the _____ of most of Potiphar's possessions.

## Down:
2. You could say that Joseph was put into a _____ prison.
3. Anger can escalate into _____.
4. The LORD blessed Joseph to _____.
5. Potiphar's wife asked Joseph to _____ with her.
8. The LORD caused the prison _____ to make Joseph a leader.
9. The LORD showed _____ toward Joseph.
11. _____ thought Joseph was a great manager of his household.
12. Egypt was considered to be _____ from where Joseph had lived.
14. An _____ named Potiphar bought Joseph from merchants.
15. Another word for grace is _____. [2]
18. If Joseph had given in to Mrs. Potiphar, he would have committed _____.
20. We could say that Mrs. Potiphar's _____ Joseph.
23. Egypt is _____ of Joseph's homeland.
25. Joseph was of _____ descent.
28. Mrs. Potiphar kept Joseph's _____ to show to her husband.
29. Mercy means loving _____. [3]
32. This story doesn't mention other _____ in Potiphar's house.
35. One story of Mrs. Potiphar was that Joseph was there to _____ them.
37. _____ merchants took Joseph to Egypt.
38. Mrs. Potiphar would not take _____ for an answer.
39. Most of the verses in this chapter begin with _____.
41. This puzzle content created by tj _____.
44. The _____ was with Joseph.
47. Nothing could _____ Joseph away from his faith in God.

[1] 27A  http://www.blueletterbible.org
[2] 15D  ibid;
[3] 29D  ibid

## Joseph Interprets Pharaoh's Dreams,
## Genesis 40-41,
## (KJV)

**(Read numbers from left to right, line by line, to find correct spaces for answers)**

# Joseph Interprets Pharaoh's Dreams,
## Genesis 40-41, (KJV)

**Across:**

4. A famine would _____ the land.
5. The interpretation of the two prisoner's dreams came _____.
7. A conjunction.
10. Rank in this story means _____. [1]
12. The butler was _____ to his old position in the king's palace.
14. The vine in the butler's dream meant _____.
18. The _____ prison was in the captain of the guard's house.
19. After a long while, the butler who'd been in prison with Joseph _____ remembered him.
20. Puzzle content by _____ johnson.
23. Seven years of _____ preceded the famine.
24. Joseph said that he was _____ from the land of his people.
29. The butler and the baker were _____ among their staff.
30. Joseph _____ to the two prisoners about their dreams.
31. 'And' can be interpreted to mean plus, additional, or _____.
34. A form of to be.
35. _____ years after the butler left prison, he remembered Joseph.
37. The baker's dream was three baskets of _____ on his head.
38. The king's title: _____.
40. In the king's dream, he was standing by the banks of a _____.
44. Lean-fleshed also described as _____. [2]
46. Joseph told Pharaoh that God would provide the _____ to his dream.

47. The fat-fleshed kine were said to be _____ looking. [3]
48. The branches that the butler dreamed of represented three _____.
51. Pharaoh's _____ usually held wine.
52. Joseph asked the butler to show _____ and remember him to the king.
55. Joseph met the butler and the _____ in prison.
56. (Con't from 1D) The man from one Down would _____ the land.
57. Jacob's favorite son.
60. Pharaoh's _____ was a warning about God's plan for Egypt.
61. Eating of baked goods was symbolic of eating the baker's _____.
63. Baked meats are _____ goods.
64. A _____ was also the cupbearer.

**Down:**

1. Joseph advised Pharaoh to find a wise and _____ man, (to 56A).
2. Joseph _____ himself up before appearing before the king.
3. According to Joseph, interpretation of dreams were of _____.
6. The lean-fleshed kine were said to be _____.
8. In the baker's dream the _____ ate the contents of the basket on his head.
9. A kine is a _____. [4]
11. None of the king's _____ could interpret his dream.
13. The thin corn was blasted by an _____ wind.

(Continued on page 55)

## A Man of Dreams

Even as a young lad,
Joseph had a Special Gift;
He dreamed Big Dreams.


His brothers called him 'Dreamer.'
His Attitude and Actions
set him Above and Ahead of
the others,
Which contributed to the
Decision they made to
Sell him to slave traders.


While in Jail,
Joseph interpreted Dreams,
which was the reason
He was called upon one day
to deduce the Dreams
Of the Pharaoh.


Pharaoh's magicians
could not analyze or surmise
the meaning of Pharaoh's Dreams.
Then!  The butler remembered
Joseph, a fellow inmate, who
had perceptively proved the dreams of
Himself, and the baker.


Right up front,
Joseph said to Pharaoh:
'It is not me,
But God…
Who gives answers to Dreams.'


Nevertheless, Pharaoh
rewarded Joseph handsomely;
He appointed him second in command
of all of his property,
because Pharaoh was pleased
With God's Answer.

## Joseph Interprets Pharaoh's Dreams,
## Genesis 40-41, (KJV)

**(Down: Continued from page 53):**

15. Two men in _____ had a dream that bothered them.
16. The _____ kine ate the fat kine.
17. Pharaoh was advised to save a _____ of all the grain during the plenteous years.
21. Joseph was _____ and fair in his dealing with the prisoners.
22. Blasted in this story means _____ or withered (v6). [5]
25. Is, _____, and will be.
26. The stored grain would keep the land from _____ during the famine.
27. The butler _____ about Joseph's request until much later.
28. God showed _____ towards Joseph.
32. The thin ears _____ the good ears.
33. In Pharaoh's dream, one could not _____ that the ill-favored kine ate the fat kine.
36. Ears, in this passage translate as _____. [6]

39. The baker's fate was _____.
41. To be imprisoned is to be _____.
42. Pharaoh's dream foretold a _____ in Egypt.
43. Corn is translated to mean _____. [7]
45. Pharaoh's dream was _____ to emphasize that it was of God.
49. To be wroth means to be _____. [8]
50. Pharaoh dreamed a _____ dream.
53. In Pharaoh's dream there were _____ kine, and the same number of ears of corn.
54. "_____ within three days shall Pharaoh lift up thy head..." (40:19).
58. Joseph's nationality was _____.
59. The butler dreamed of a vine with _____ branches.
62. Unhappy can be described as being _____.

[1-8] Wayne A. Brindle, et al. eds. *The King James Study Bible* (Lynchburg, VA: Liberty University, 1988) pp. 40-42

## Pharaoh Promotes Joseph
## Genesis 41:37-57; 47:11-31, (KJV)

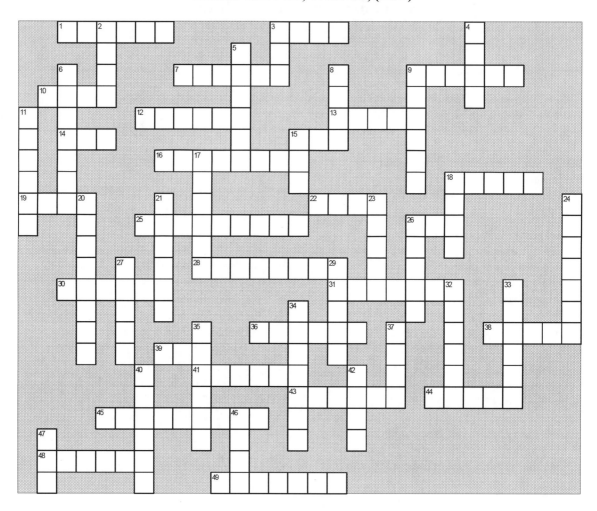

**Across: (Hint: Number of blanks doesn't necessarily indicate number of letters in answer)**   .

1.  Joseph's sons were born _ _ _ _ _ _ the famine.
3.  Pharaoh told Joseph there was none so _ _ _ _ as him.
7.  Joseph was _ _ _ _ _ years old when he stood before Pharaoh.
9.  The king was impressed with Joseph and put him in _ _ _ _ _ _ of practically everything.
10. Joseph _ _ _ _ food from the store houses when the people came to him.
12. Dearth translates as _ _ _ _ _ _.[1]
13. The king gave Joseph clothes of _ _ _ _ _ to wear.
14. Joseph was given a _ _ _ _ name.
15. Connects phrases when writing or speaking.
16. Joseph's second son's name translates as _ _ _ _ _, (Gen 41:52).[2]
18. The famine _ _ _ _ _ sore in the land.
19. When the people had no more livestock to sell, they sold their _ _ _ _ for food.
22. Joseph gave his father and brothers the _ _ _ _ of everything.
25. Cattle are the same as _ _ _ _ _ _.[3]
26. A word that warns of a difference.

**Pharaoh Promotes Joseph, (Across: Continued from prior page):**

28. The people eventually sold themselves as _ _ _ _ _ _ _ _ of Pharaoh.
30. On the _ _ _ _ _ _ only, was Pharaoh greater than Joseph.
31. The second son of Joseph was _ _ _ _ _ _ _.
36. Jacob was the father of the tribes of _ _ _ _ _ _, (Gen 49:16).
38. The people were required to give a _ _ _ _ _ of their crop yield to Pharaoh.
39. Joseph fathered _ _ _ _ _ _ sons in Egypt.
41. It was a very _ _ _ _ _ _ famine.
43. Joseph rode in the king's _ _ _ _ _ _ chariot.
44. Because of Joseph's management, Pharaoh became owner of most of the land in _ _ _ _ _.
45. Everything that Joseph did _ _ _ _ _ _.
48. Joseph's _ _ _ _ _ _ _ to the king landed him the job as overseer of Egypt.
49. The wife of Joseph was _ _ _ _ _ .

**Down:**

2. Joseph's brothers came to Egypt looking for _ _ _ _ _.
3. Without asking _ _ _ _, Joseph accepted his blessings.
4. '_ _ _ _ me not in the land of Egypt,' was a request of Jacob.
5. Joseph's father-in-law was a _ _ _ _ _ _.
6. This puzzle content designed by tj _ _ _ _ _ _.
8. Pharaoh placed a _ _ _ _ chain on Joseph's neck.
9. Not only Egypt, but _ _ _ _ _ _ also was affected by the famine.
11. One thing people exchanged for food was _ _ _ _ _ .
15. Joseph was ruler over _ _ _ _ of Egypt.
17. No one would do anything _ _ _ _ _ _ they checked with Joseph first.
18. The Lord was _ _ _ _ Joseph.
20. Pharaoh gave Joseph Potipherah's _ _ _ _ _ _ _ _ as wife.
21. The king also gave Joseph his _ _ _ _ _ _ ring.
23. To put one's hand under another's _ _ _ _ _ was a guarantee of one's word.
24. _ _ _ _ _ allotted food to the priests.
26. The people of Egypt cried to Pharaoh for _ _ _ _ _.
27. All the people _ _ _ _ _ down to Joseph.
29. After the plentiful years came _ _ _ _ _ years of famine, as predicted.
32. Joseph's first son was Manasseh, meaning _ _ _ _ _ _ to forget. (hint: with 'ing'). [4]
33. Pharaoh recognized that the _ _ _ _ _ _ of God was in Joseph.
34. The land of the _ _ _ _ _ _ _ was not sold.
35. The place where Jacob lived in Egypt.
37. Joseph gave the people _ _ _ _ to sow in their new land.
40. The food was _ _ _ _ _ _ in order to provide for the lean years to come.
42. Everything that Joseph did turned out to be _ _ _ _ _ _.
46. Joseph's plan was good in the _ _ _ _ _ _ of Pharaoh.
47. Joseph made a new _ _ _ in Egypt about the percentage of crops to be given to Pharaoh.

---

[1, 2, 4]    Brindle, Wayne T., et al, eds. *The King James Study Bible* (Lynchburg, VA: Liberty University, 1988),    p. 83

[3]    http://www.blueletterbible.org

# Joseph's Brothers In Egypt, Genesis 42, (KJV)

**(Numbers read from left to right, line by line, horizontally, to find answer spaces)**

**Joseph's Brothers In Egypt, (Continued):**

**Across:**

4. Reuben's offer to sacrifice his children was _____.
9. Joseph used an _____ to speak with his brothers.
11. His brothers referred to Joseph as "my _____".
13. Joseph chose _____ to hold in prison until his brothers returned.
14. When the brothers found _____ in their bags, they were afraid.
15. Joseph accused his brothers of being _____.
16. Reuben offered _____ of his sons as a sacrifice in order to prove his word.
17. The same as jail or prison.
18. Jacob was _____ sending his youngest to Egypt.
19. Another word for no.
21. _____ is the writer of Genesis.
23. The ten brothers referred to themselves as Joseph's _____.
26. One brother was not allowed to return home; he was _____ and put in prison.
27. Joseph's brothers regretted their terrible _____ against him, (to 6D).
29. Another term for recompense is _____ back.
30. Upon recognizing them, Joseph spoke _____ to his brothers.
31. Joseph was mistaken to be an _____.
33. He was the one who had pleaded with the others not to kill Joseph.
35. A food staple in Egypt.
37. Joseph sold grain to all the _____.
38. Pharaoh made Joseph _____ of Egypt.
42. Joseph knew his brothers; but they didn't _____ him.
44. The _____ was evident throughout the land.
45. Joseph accused them of coming to see the _____ of the land.
47. Genesis is one book of the _____.
48. Many of the verses in this chapter begin with the word _____.
49. Joseph did not _____ grain to his brothers.

**Down:**

1. Severely or _____, (v7). [1]
2. This many brothers went to Egypt for food.
3. Joseph's family traveled from _____.
5. The brothers called themselves _____ men.
6. (From 27A)...they felt they were being _____ for their behavior years before.
7. The _____ he'd had when he was young came back to Joseph.
8. Considering death for his children was a _____ gesture for Reuben.
10. Reuben offered his sons' life as a pledge of his _____.
12. Another word for food, (ch 14:11). [2]
20. Joseph's brothers bowed to him with their _____ to the earth.
21. Jacob was afraid some _____ might befall Benjamin.
22. Worry and grief is what Jacob said would cause his hair to _____.
23. After Pharaoh, Joseph was _____ in command.
24. Feeling ashamed, Joseph's brothers finally admitted their _____ concerning him.
25. As he listened to his brother's discuss their past behavior, Joseph _____.
28. It was his idea to sell Joseph to traveling merchants. (ch 37:26-27)
32. Joseph required that their younger brother come to Egypt to _____ that they were not spies.
34. This puzzle composed by _____.
36. Joseph put his brothers in prison for _____ days.
37. Joseph and his youngest brother had the same _____.
39. "...and _____ is not." (v13)
40. Joseph had _____ half-brothers.
41. Both Jacob and his sons were _____ to keep the money they found.
43. "What is this that _____ has done unto us?"
46. Joseph put each man's money in their _____ of grain.

## Food, Gifts, Tears
## Genesis 43 - 45 (KJV)

**Clues: (Ch is used for Chapter of same book; V is for Verse of puzzle chapter.)**

Jacob was elated because Joseph was still _____
Joseph was _____ only to Pharaoh
Jacob didn't want him to go to Egypt
_____ told Joseph to bring his family to Egypt

Served at noon
The name of the promised land: _____
He emerged as the spokesman: _____
Welfare refers to well _____

Places for eating were set according to _____
Egyptians did not ____ with Hebrews
Israel was pleased to go to _____ because of Joseph
Joseph became _____ when he recognized Benjamin

Joseph, _____ of Egypt
He was held as a hostage: _____
Another word for sore, _____
____ be unto you--Fear not

Benjamin's food was _____ times that of his brothers
'It was not you that sent me to Egypt but ____'
The men fell before Joseph on the _____
Bowels in this story translates as _____, (ch 43:30) [2]

Puzzle content by TJ _____
Same as security deposit: _____
Translation for posterity: _____ [4]
Ch 43, Jacob or _____ [3]

Joseph finally revealed his identity to his brothers
In Genesis 45:18, fat refers to ? [1]
_____ in Genesis 45:8 refers to ruler or chief
Among other gifts, they discovered double _____ in their bags

Joseph sent to Egypt to _____ life
Joseph ate _____ with his brothers
He put a _____ cup in one bag

Seeing his brothers caused Joseph to _____
The brothers brought gifts of honey, spices and _____ to Joseph
It was customary to give water to drink and to wash a guest's _____
Joseph was a _____ for many years before God made him a leader
Pharaoh sent _____ to ease Joseph's family's travel to Egypt

Joseph twice returned the _____ his brothers brought back to him
Pharaoh promised the good of the _____ to Joseph's family, (ch 45:17)
His brothers and father referred to Joseph as ____ ____ (Gen 43:6-7)(2 wds)
His brothers feared being called thieves because of _____ in their bags

[1-4]    Wayne A. Brindle, et al. eds., *The King James Study Bible* (Lynchburg, VA: Liberty University, 1988),   pp. 85-89

**Food, Gifts, Tears**
**Genesis 43 - 45 (KJV)**

Find answers to clues listed on the previous page and circle the words in the grid.  Words can go across, down, and in three diagonals.  You may find words that are not scripted, and some that appear more than once.

```
N  G  N  C  A  N  A  A  N  R  G  F  N  L  N  N  L  E  L  V
J  I  K  H  S  G  O  V  E  R  N  O  R  M  K  V  V  A  G  R
G  M  S  R  E  I  T  G  O  D  N  T  M  G  K  R  T  X  N  C
R  F  H  R  T  A  L  J  M  O  N  E  Y  R  E  N  Y  Z  Y  D
O  T  Q  A  A  N  R  V  M  F  K  T  W  S  Z  U  F  V  T  L
U  P  E  Q  X  E  W  T  E  H  T  P  E  W  N  T  G  N  A  R
N  B  F  T  W  T  L  W  C  R  E  R  F  T  R  S  A  N  F  N
D  L  K  J  K  C  X  N  C  E  P  G  M  D  N  V  O  S  A  Y
M  O  N  E  Y  Z  U  B  W  K  L  T  T  I  R  I  N  I  T  J
A  T  C  H  H  L  N  B  E  I  N  G  M  E  T  A  S  M  H  O
L  F  S  P  M  L  L  Z  V  D  W  A  S  O  M  N  T  E  E  H
I  E  E  H  N  H  K  F  N  Q  J  M  M  E  O  L  T  O  R  N
V  E  V  A  R  N  M  O  V  N  B  E  H  G  L  L  B  N  M  S
E  T  E  R  Q  E  C  V  E  H  D  T  A  L  J  U  D  A  H  O
S  H  R  A  P  E  M  B  H  M  T  W  M  E  U  N  G  M  B  N
K  U  E  O  S  E  F  N  J  O  S  E  P  H  G  N  D  L  E  K
V  B  R  H  Z  D  A  I  A  H  Q  F  D  L  M  Y  C  P  S  H
T  K  T  E  W  K  T  C  V  N  P  R  J  H  Q  L  P  H  T  D
M  T  N  D  T  Y  T  F  E  E  T  M  O  N  E  Y  R  T  J  W
B  Q  L  X  L  Y  V  T  Q  R  B  I  R  T  H  R  I  G  H  T
```

## Jacob Prepares To Die,
### Genesis 48, 49, (KJV)

**(Ch is used for Chapter of same book; V is for Verse of puzzle reference chapter.)**

**Across:**
1.  God appeared to Jacob in _____, later called Bethel.
3.  There is prophecy in Ch 49:10-11 which points to _____.
7.  Ephraim was to become _____ than his brother.
10.  The promise made to Jacob is like the promise God made to _____.
11.  A _____ can be described as a rod, staff, or branch; a mark of authority, (ch 49:10). [1]
12.  Judah is said to be like a _____.
14.  Future sons of Joseph would _____ from their father, and not their grandfather.
15.  _____ is to become a judge.
17.  God promised this land to Jacob and his seed.
18.  Joseph's mother _____ in Canaan.
21.  Human seed refers to _____, (plural).
23.  This puzzle content designed by _____ Johnson.
29.  Beautiful words compare Naphtali to a loose _____.
31.  Dan is also said to be an adder or _____ which bites the horse's heels.
33.  Issachar is said to be a strong _____.
35.  Israel referred to Reuben as the beginning of his _____.
36.  The archers bitterly _____ Joseph.
37.  Jacob's _____ was for the grandson upon whom he laid his right hand.
40.  Buried in the cave at Mamre: the bones of Abraham, Sarah, Isaac, Rebekah, and _____.
42.  Asher is to produce rich _____, and royal dainties.
44.  Benjamin was to be as a ravenous _____, devouring and dividing the prey.
45.  Joseph's mother was _____.
46.  Jacob told his sons their future of the _____ days.
48.  Portion in 48:22 literally means _____. [2]
50.  Jacob charged his sons to bury him in the _____ of Machpelah, in the land of Canaan.
51.  Simeon and Levi were said to be instruments of _____.
53.  Jacob treated Joseph's sons as his _____ sons.
55.  To collect one's strength is to _____ oneself.
56.  Reuben would not excel because he _____ his father's wife.

**Down:**
2.  Between two burdens translates to be _____. [3]
4.  Simeon and Levi were to be divided and _____.
5.  Gad literally means a _____, which will overcome him.

(Clues continued on page 65)

## Jacob Prepares To Die, Genesis 48, 49, (KJV)

**(Numbers read from left to right, line by line, horizontally, either Across or Down.)**

## Jacob Dies in Egypt

---

Jacob died;
and Joseph made preparations
to carry his father's remains
back to Canaan,
to bury in the cave
that his great grandfather Abraham
had purchased years before.


All the sons of Jacob
carried him to Canaan,
and buried him in the cave
in the field of Machpelah,
which his ancestor bought for
a burying place
from Ephron, the Hittite.


Jacob lived to be
one hundred forty-seven years old,
He died in Egypt.


(from Genesis 47:28; 49:33; 50:13)

## Jacob Prepares To Die,
## Genesis 48, 49, (KJV)

### (Down: Continued from page 62)

6. The full branches of Joseph ran over the _____.
8. Hebrew for God Almighty, (2 words combined). [4]
9. Jacob was actually Ephraim and Manasseh's _____.
13. To 'yield up the ghost,' is to _____, (ch 49:33). [5]
16. In Chapter 48:16, Jacob spoke of God as an _____.
19. Jacob was old, and his eyes were _____.
20. Joseph is said to be a _____ bough.
22. Jacob prayed that his _____ be given to Joseph's two sons.
24. Jacob lived in Egypt _____ years, (ch 47:28).
25. Even though Jacob could not see well, he _____ placed his hands exactly where he intended.
26. The blessings given by Jacob _____ above, or excelled over those of his father and grandfather.
27. Israel also _____ Joseph and gave him one portion more than his brothers.
28. This son is predicted to become a slave, (ch 49:14-15).
30. Jacob laid his _____ hand on the head of Ephraim.
32. Leah was the first _____ of Jacob.
34. The first-born of Joseph was _____.
35. _____ is who the sceptre/scepter belongs to.
37. Judah's brethren would one day _____ down before him.
38. Joseph would prevail against his enemies because_____ would sustain him.
39. God chose _____ to be his people, (Ex 19:5; Lev 26:12; 1 Chr 17:7-9).
41. A _____ is called an ass in the Bible.
43. Another name for Bethlehem.
47. Jacob gave his blessings to _____ sons and two grandsons.
48. Zebulun's dwelling would be a haven for _____.
49. _____ told Joseph of his father's illness, (ch 48:2).
50. Jacob's blessings were set to be on the _____ of Joseph's head.
52. The cave and the field of Ephron was bought from the children of _____.
54. Jacob said that God _____ him and redeemed him from evil.

[1]   11A   Wyatt A. Brindle, et al. eds., *The King James Study Bible* (Lynchburg, VA: Liberty University, 1988), p. 95
[2]   48A   Ibid, p.94
[3]   2D    http://www.blueletterbible.org
[4]   8D    ibid
[5]   13D   Brindle, p. 95

## End of Days For Jacob,
## Genesis 50, (KJV)

**(Ch is used for Chapter of same book; V is used for Verse of puzzle reference chapter.)**

He purchased a cave in Canaan for a burying place

Joseph predicted that his _____ would be carried out of Egypt

Joseph fell on his father's face and _____

Horsemen and _____ were available for Joseph's journey to bury his father

When Joseph died, he also was embalmed in Egypt and put in a chest or _____, (v 26)

Abel-mizraim means mourning of _____, (v 11)

The people of Canaan thought Joseph's family to be _____, (v 11)

Old men or the aged are referred to as _____

Prior owner of the burying place where Jacob's body was to be placed

Joseph's brothers asked him for _____

There were _____ days of mourning in Egypt for Jacob

Yielding up the ghost, Jacob _____ his last breath (with an 's')(ch 49:33)

What Joseph's brothers meant for evil, God meant for _____

Jacob's family lived in the land of _____ while in Egypt

The previous owner of the cave was of _____ heredity

Land of Abraham, _____ and Jacob

He was 147 when he died (ch 47:28)

The _____ floor at Atad is beyond the Jordan, (v 11)

Joseph lived to bounce his great-grandchildren on his _____

The burying place for Jacob was the cave at _____

Egypt _____ Jacob's death along with Joseph and his family

Joseph lived in Egypt _____ years, (Gen 37:2; 50:22)

Servants of _____ also traveled to Canaan with Joseph

Joseph's servant _____ embalmed Jacob

Jacob lived in Egypt _____ years, (Gen 47:28)

Joseph was _____ years old when he was sold as a servant slave

Jacob's _____ carried him into the land of Canaan to be buried

The funeral procession mourned near Atad for _____ days

The people mourning near Atad presented a solemn and _____ lamentation

Joseph prophesied that God would surely _____ Israel to deliver them out of Egypt

Progenitor or _____ (ch 49:26)

To provide for or _____ for (v21)

Perhaps, or _____ (v15)

He was 110 when he died

Jacob desired burial in _____

Favor or _____

Creator of this puzzle

To give up the ghost; _____

# End of Days For Jacob,
## Genesis 50
### (KJV)

The puzzle grid contains answers to the clues on the previous page. Figure out what words the clues represent, and circle the words in the grid. Words can share one letter; go down, across, and in three diagonals. Various unscripted words may be found in the grid, and words may appear more than once.

```
C  N  M  K  V  Z  K  P  H  Y  S  I  C  I  A  N  S  L  J  N  F
R  I  P  T  G  C  R  C  T  L  B  R  E  A  T  H  E  S  D  S  M
H  N  F  T  F  R  G  O  S  H  E  N  W  J  P  R  L  O  P  E  T
R  E  O  J  R  H  A  C  O  F  F  I  N  W  H  Y  O  X  E  V  H
Y  T  R  K  K  R  T  C  N  T  H  X  R  R  E  G  J  C  R  E  L
B  Y  G  P  P  Q  J  T  E  J  T  T  F  K  G  P  L  N  A  N  K
V  T  I  L  H  Q  P  C  X  I  O  L  N  M  R  N  T  H  D  J  M
B  H  V  Q  K  Y  P  T  S  L  H  S  N  N  M  N  E  T  V  M  B
Q  R  E  F  G  B  R  I  V  O  C  M  E  N  Q  I  D  K  E  R  T
G  E  N  E  Z  K  V  B  A  L  A  R  C  P  D  K  G  D  N  D  W
S  E  E  T  T  M  N  R  P  D  N  B  V  H  H  B  R  Z  T  K  Z
E  E  S  H  N  E  A  E  F  L  A  T  R  V  A  O  O  E  U  B  L
V  G  S  T  T  H  P  V  E  K  A  H  Y  A  T  R  R  N  R  L  Z
E  Y  H  H  P  G  J  H  R  S  N  T  W  S  H  O  I  S  E  B  V
N  P  I  R  K  M  M  N  R  L  R  B  E  Y  S  A  T  O  O  S  R
T  T  T  E  T  Q  O  D  F  O  O  C  B  N  D  M  M  R  T  N  H
E  I  T  S  W  W  U  B  F  C  N  O  U  R  I  S  H  V  H  S  S
E  A  I  H  R  T  R  D  A  A  T  M  S  E  V  E  N  T  E  E  N
N  N  T  I  L  X  N  J  R  M  T  J  J  O  H  N  S  O  N  K  M
L  S  E  N  T  B  E  K  M  A  C  H  P  E  L  A  H  W  Y  G  P
J  K  M  G  T  L  D  I  S  A  A  C  E  L  D  E  R  S  P  H  K
```

~ NOTES ~

# Chapter & Verse

## Puzzle Solutions

APPENDIX A

## People and Characters
## In Genesis
### Various Scripture

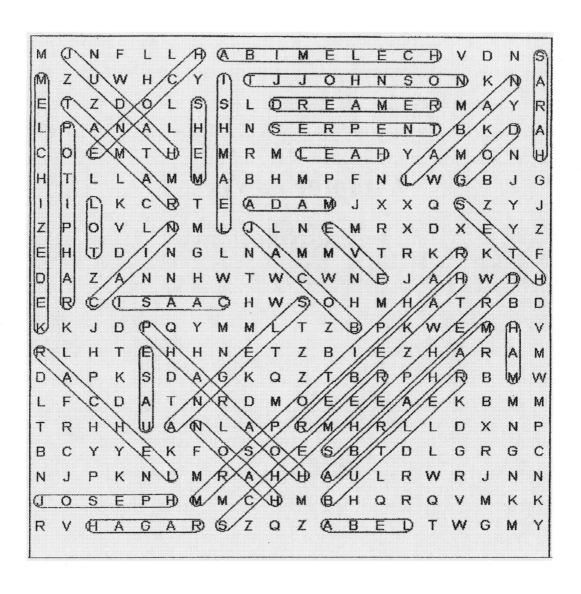

## Places & Cases in Genesis
### Various Scripture (KJV)

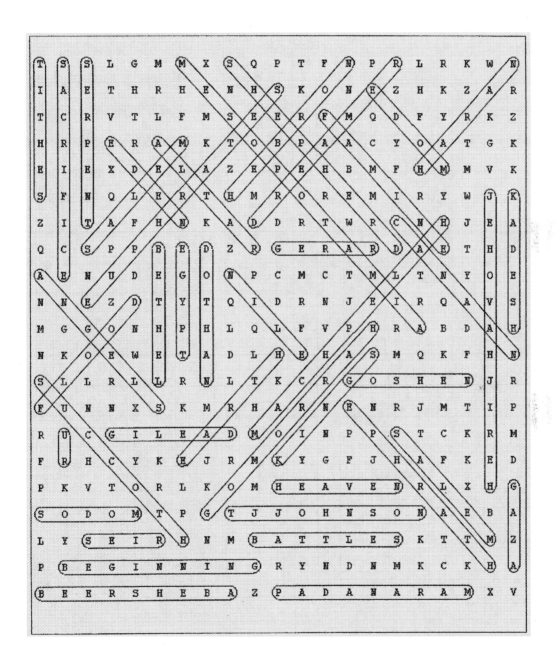

## God's Promises to Abram/Abraham
### Genesis 12:1-13, 14:18;
### 15:1-6, 12-13
### (KJV)

**Faith, Hope, Trust**
**Believing God's Promises**
**Genesis 12:1-9; Heb 11:1-3, (KJV)**

A 5

# Battle of the Kings
## Genesis 14
### (KJV)

## Abraham and Abimelech
## Genesis 20
## (KJV)

# Isaac & Abimelech
## Genesis 26
## (KJV)

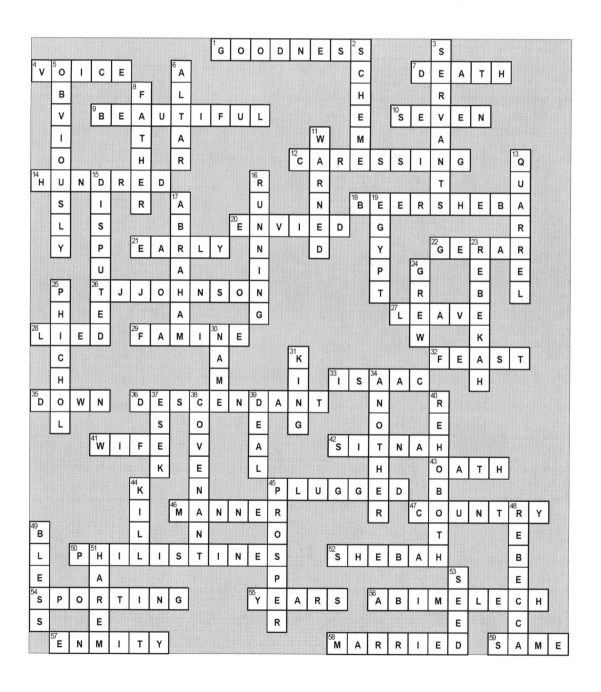

# Birthrights & Blessings
## Genesis 27 – 28
### (KJV)

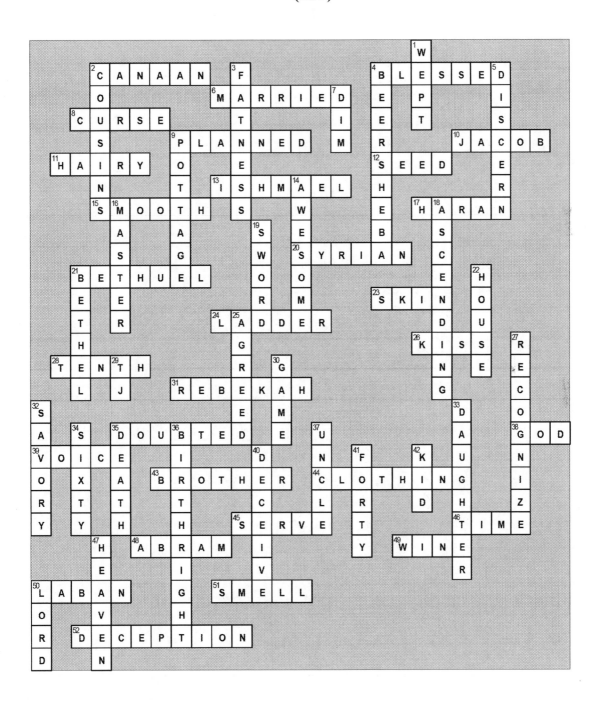

## Jacob Chooses a Bride
## Genesis 29
## (KJV)

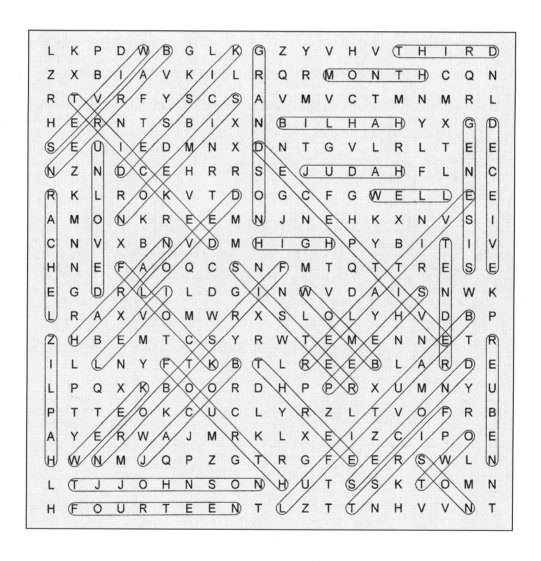

**Jacob's Family**
**Genesis 29:31-35; & Chapter 30**
**(KJV)**

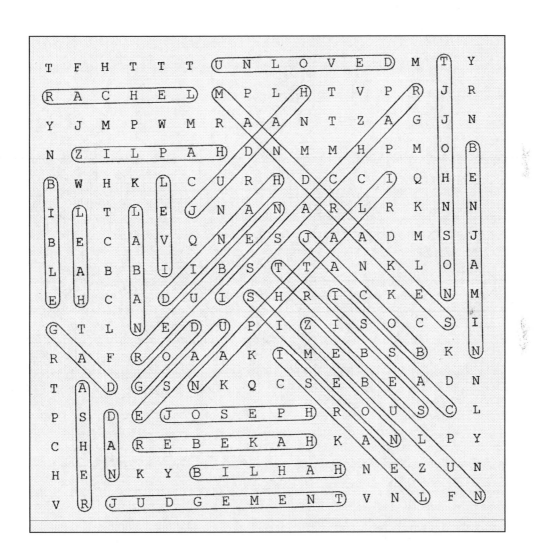

## Trickery Among Men,
## Goats, & Sheep
## Genesis 30:25-43
## (KJV)

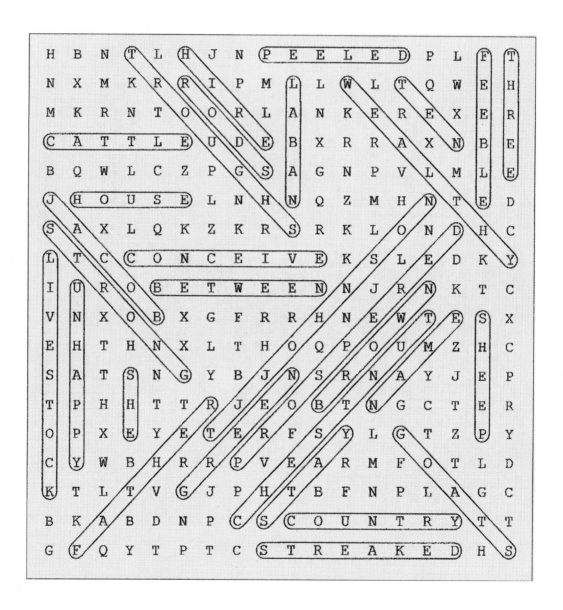

**Jacob Leaves Laban**
**Genesis 31 & 32,**
**(KJV)**

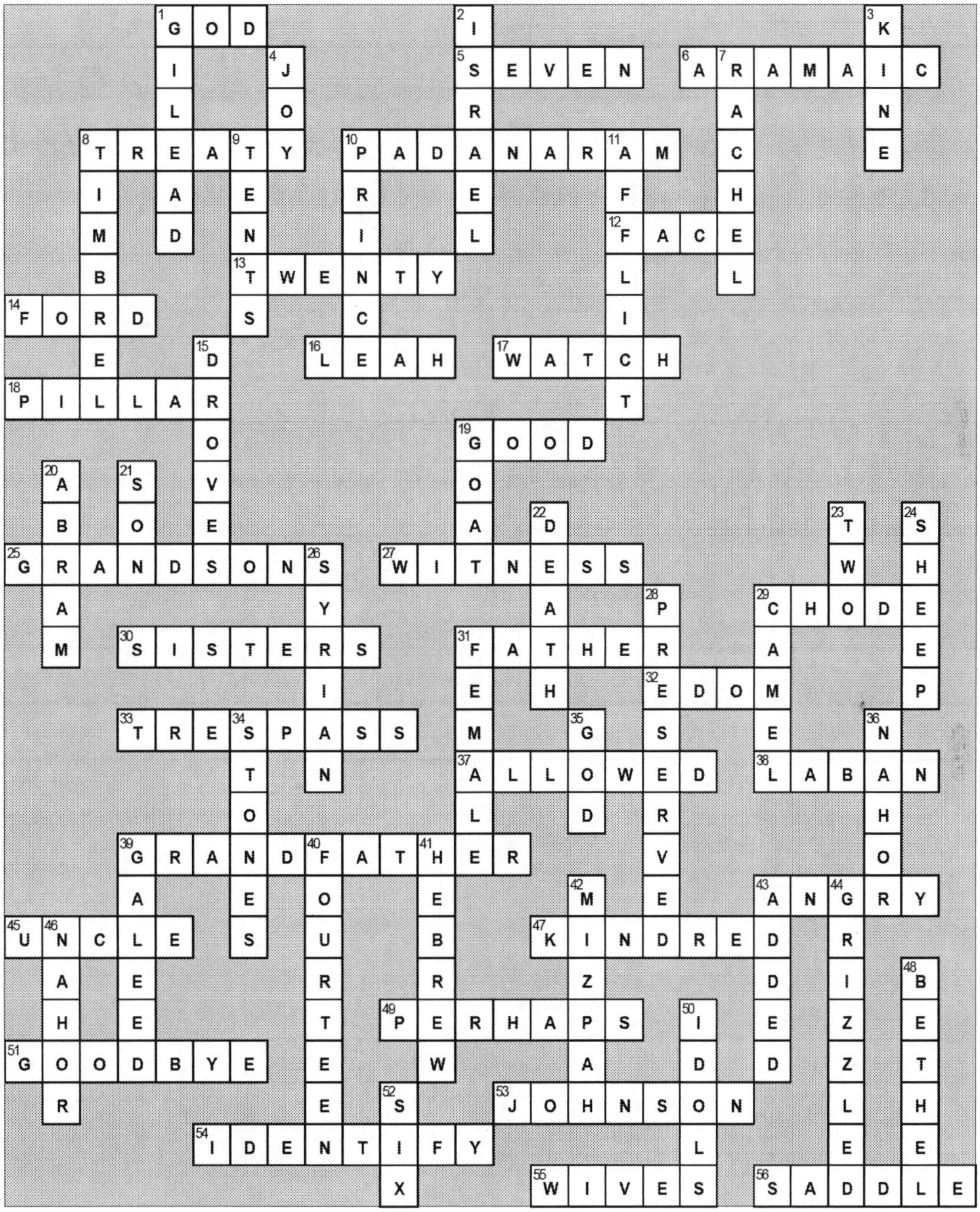
1 GOD
2 I
3 K
4 J
5 SEVEN
6 A 7 RAMAIC
8 TREA 9 TY
10 PADANAR 11 AM
12 FACE
13 TWENTY
14 FORD
15 D
16 LEAH
17 WATCH
18 PILLAR
19 GOOD
20 A
21 S
22 D
23 T
24 S
25 GRANDSON 26 S
27 WITNESS
28 P
29 CHODE
30 SISTERS
31 FATHER
32 EDOM
33 TRE 34 SPASS
35 G
36 N
37 ALLOWED
38 LABAN
39 GRAND 40 FAT 41 HER
42 M
43 AN 44 GRY
45 U 46 NCLE
47 KINDRED
48 B
49 PERHAPS
50 I
51 GOODBYE
52 S
53 JOHNSON
54 IDENTIFY
55 WIVES
56 SADDLE

**Meeting Esau Again, (22)**
**Genesis 32 & 33**
**(KJV)**

**Dinah's Dilemma**
**Genesis 34 & 35**
**(KJV)**

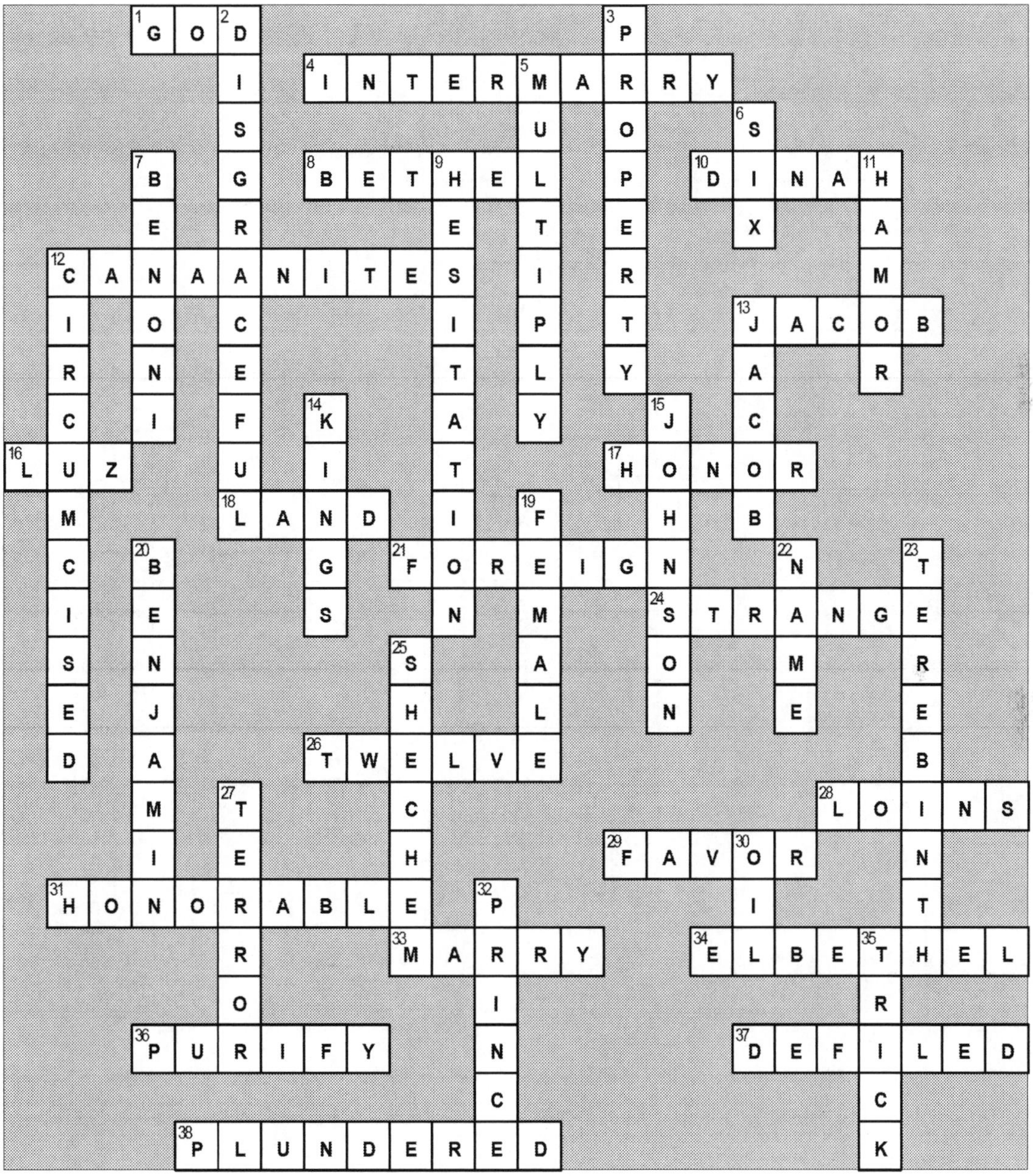

# The Dreamer
## Genesis 37:1-11
### (KJV)

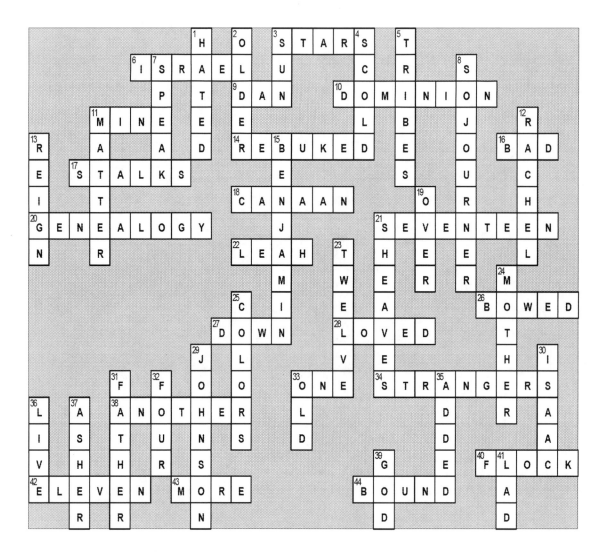

## Plot To Kill Joseph
## Genesis 37:11-36,
## (KJV)

# Sons of Judah
## Genesis 38, (KJV)

## Judah And Tamar
### Genesis 38, (KJV)

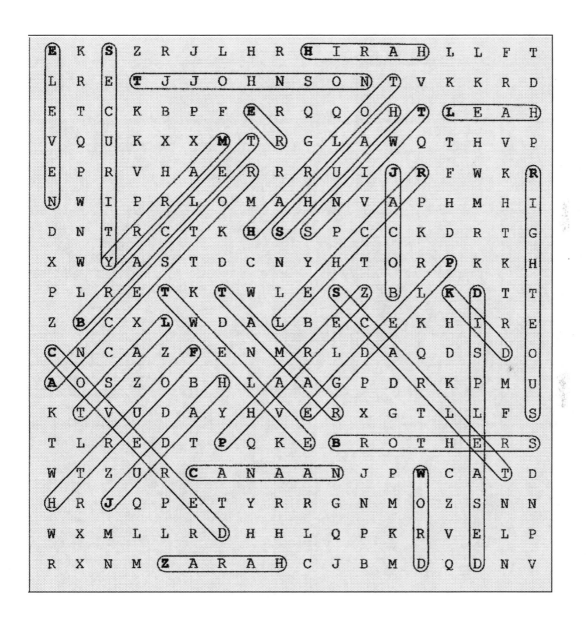

# In Potiphar's House
## Genesis 39
## (KJV)

# Joseph Interprets Pharaoh's Dreams, Genesis 40-41, (KJV)

Across:

4. CONSUME
5. TRUE
7. AND
10. PLUMP
12. RESTORED
14. GRAPES
18. KINGS
19. FINALLY
23. PLENTY
24. STOLEN
29. CHIEF
30. SPOKE
31. ALSO
35. TWO
37. BREAD
38. PHARAOH
40. RIVER
44. GAUNT
46. ANSWER
47. FINE
48. DAYS
51. CUP
52. KINDNESS
55. BAKER
56. OVERSEE
57. JOSEPH
60. DREAM
61. FLESH
63. BAKED
64. BUTLER

Down:

1. DICERN
2. CLE
3. GODDERN
6. UGLY
8. BIN
9. C
11. MAGICIANS
13. EADS
15. PRISON
16. SKIN
17. FIFTH
20. TUS
21. J
22. BIG
25. WAS
26. PR
27. FRGT
28. FLVE
32. A
33. TEED
34. IS
36. H
39. HANGING
41. INCARD
42. F
43. G
45. REPE
49. ANGGY
50. SECCND
53. SEEVEN
54. Y
55. BTE
58. HBRW
59. THRE
62. S

# Pharaoh Promotes Joseph
## Genesis 41:37-57; 47:11-31
### (KJV)

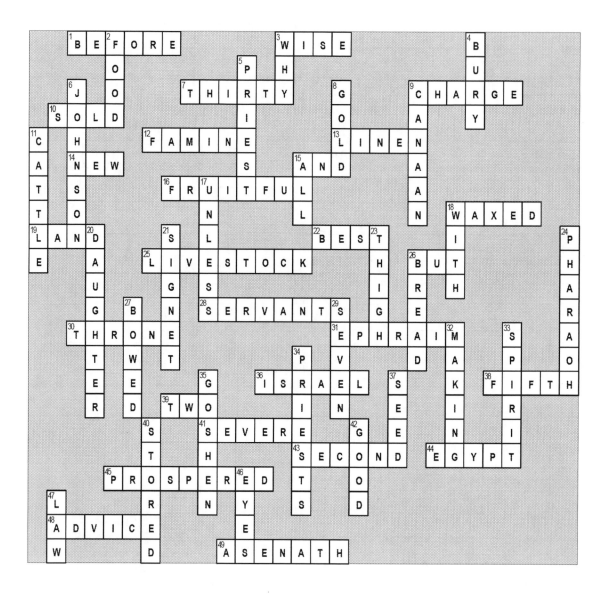

**Joseph's Brothers In Egypt**
**Genesis 42, (KJV)**

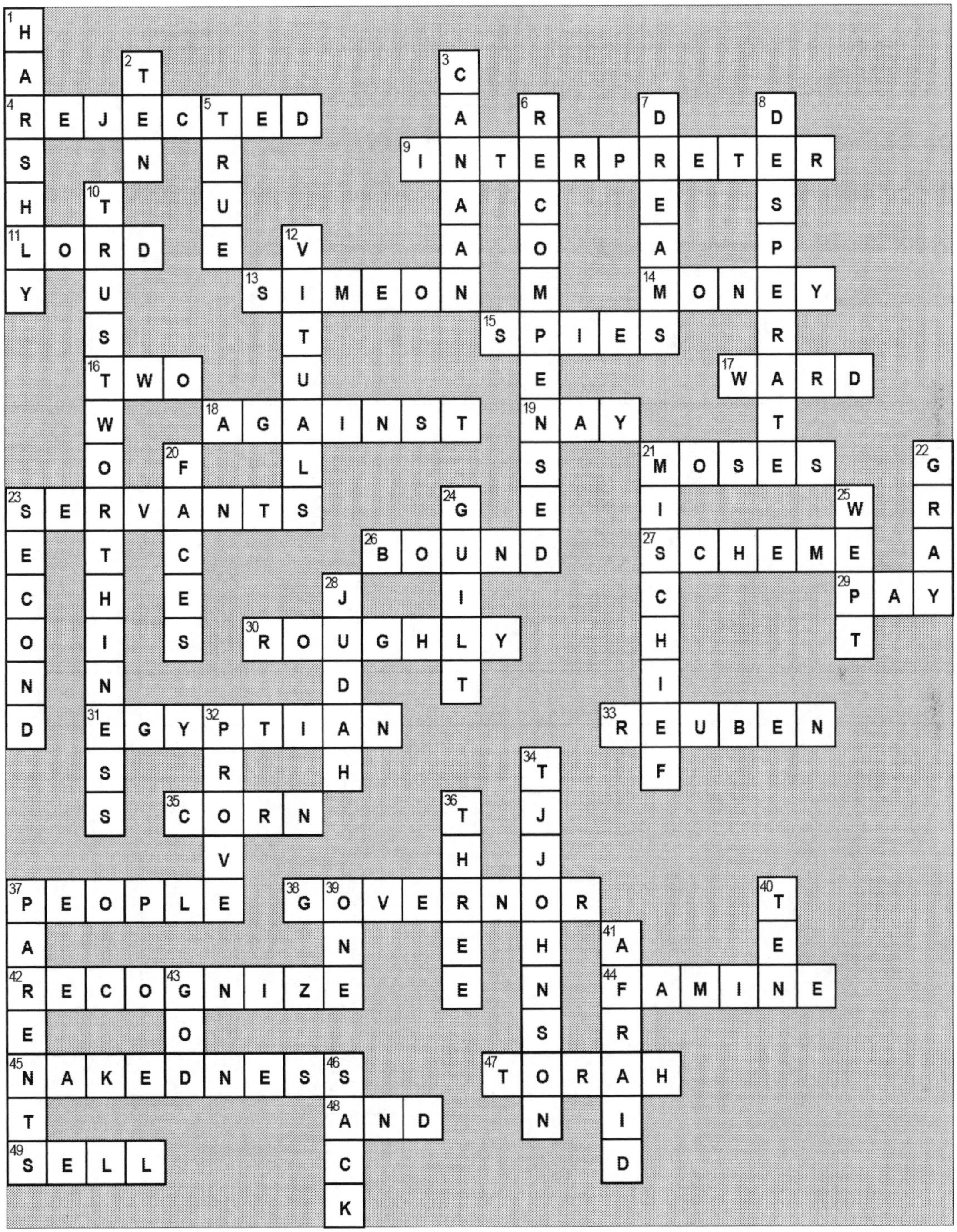
4 REJECTED
9 INTERPRETER
11 LORD
13 SIMEON
14 MONEY
15 SPIES
16 TWO
17 WARD
18 AGAINST
19 NAY
21 MOSES
23 SERVANTS
26 BOUND
27 SCHEME
29 PAY
30 ROUGHLY
31 EGYPTIAN
33 REUBEN
35 CORN
37 PEOPLE
38 GOVERNOR
42 RECOGNIZE
44 FAMINE
45 NAKEDNESS
47 TORAH
48 AND
49 SELL
1 HARSHLY
2 TEN
3 CANAAN
5 TRUE
6 RECOMPENSED
7 DREAMS
8 DESPERATE
10 TRUSTWORTHINESS
12 VITUALS
20 FACES
21 MISCHIEF
22 GRAY
23 SECOND
24 GUILT
25 WEPT
28 JUDAH
32 PROVE
34 TJJOHNSON
36 THREE
37 PARENT
39 ONE
40 TEN
41 AFRAID
43 GO
46 SACK

# Food, Gifts, & Tears
## Genesis 43-45,
## (KJV)

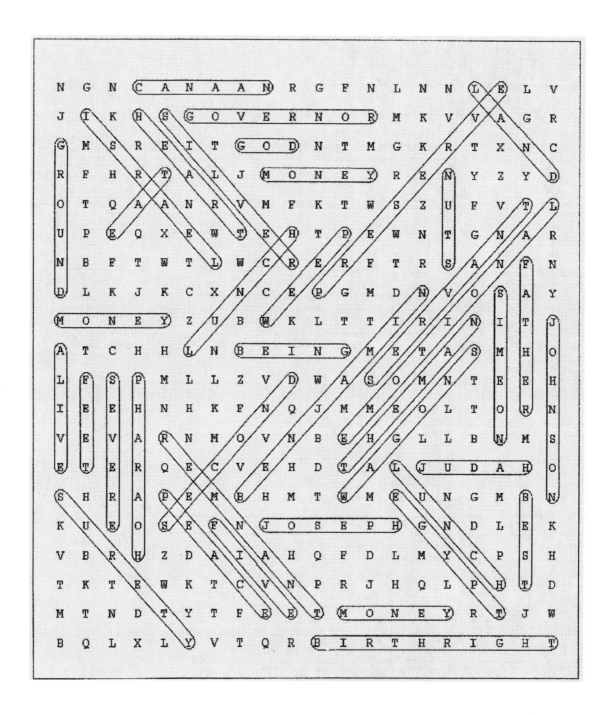

## Jacob Prepares To Die,
## Genesis 48, 49, (KJV)

1 LUZ
3 JESUS
7 GREATER
10 ABRAHAM
11 SCEPTER
12 LION
14 INHERIT
15 DAN
17 CANAAN
18 DIED
21 DESCENDANTS
23 TJ
29 DEER
31 SERPENT
33 ASS
35 STRENGTH
36 HATE
37 BLESSING
40 LEAH
42 BREAD
44 WOLF
45 RACHEL
46 LAST
48 SHOULDER
50 CAVE
51 CRUELTY
53 OWN
55 STRENGTHEN
56 DEFILED
2 UNCERTAIN
4 SCATTERED
5 TROOP
6 WALL
8 ELSHADDAI
9 GRANDFATHER
13 DIE
16 ANGEL
19 DIM
20 FRUITFUL
22 NAM
24 SEVENTEEN
25 WITTINGLY
26 PREVAILED
27 BLESSED
28 ISSACHAR
30 RIGHT
32 WIFE
34 MANASSE
35 SHILOH
37 BOW
38 GOD
39 ISRAEL
41 DONKEY
43 EPHRATH
47 TWELVE
48 SHIP
49 ONE
50 CROWN
52 HETH
54 FED

## End of Days for Jacob
## Genesis 50
## (KJV)

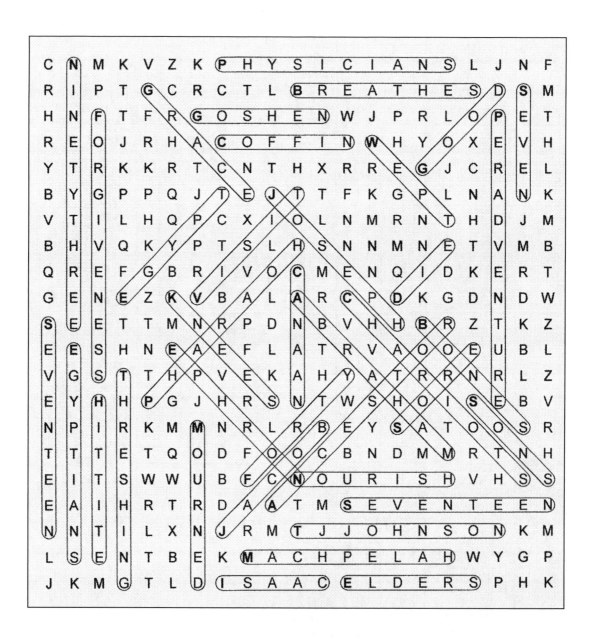

**Bibliography:**

Brindle, Wayne A., et al, eds. The King James Study Bible. Lynchburg: VA, Liberty University, 1988.

http://www.blueletterbible.org, 1994-2007.

Unger, Merrill F. Unger's Bible Dictionary. Third Edition. Chicago: Moody, 1957.

Bryant, Alton T., ed. The New Compact Bible Dictionary. Grand Rapids, MI: Zondervan, 1967.

Chapter & Verse

~ NOTES ~

*Please address comments on website:* www.hayneskid.com